V63.W26 S75 2012

Promotion or the bottom of the river

:

33663004848202

NRG

DATE DUE

Promotion *or the*
Bottom of the River

Studies in Maritime History
William N. Still, Jr., Series Editor

RECENT TITLES

PROMOTION *or the*

BOTTOM OF THE RIVER

The Blue and Gray Naval Careers of
Alexander F. Warley, South Carolinian

JOHN M. STICKNEY

The University of South Carolina Press

© 2012 University of South Carolina

Published by the University of South Carolina Press
Columbia, South Carolina 29208

www.sc.edu/uscpress

Manufactured in the United States of America

21 20 19 18 17 16 15 14 13 12   10 9 8 7 6 5 4 3 2 1

Library of Congress Cataloging-in-Publication Data

Stickney, John M. (John Monro)
    Promotion or the bottom of the river : the blue and gray naval careers of Alexander F.
Warley, South Carolinian / John M. Stickney.
        p. cm.— (Studies in maritime history)
    Includes bibliographical references and index.
    ISBN 978-1-61117-065-8 (cloth : alk. paper)
        1. Warley, Alexander F., 1823–1895. 2. United States. Navy—Officers—Biography.
3. Confederate States of America. Navy—Officers—Biography. 4. United States—
History, Naval—19th century. 5. United States—History—Civil War, 1861–1865—
Naval operations, Confederate. I. Title.
    V63.W26S75 2012
    973.7'57092—DC23
    [B]   2011044010

This book was printed on a recycled paper with 30 percent postconsumer waste content.

For Pris

Contents

ILLUSTRATIONS

Preface

Alex Warley was not any easy subject to build a book around. His gallantry was conspicuous when he was commanding the Confederate ironclad ram *Manassas* on the river below New Orleans in 1861 and 1862, and he is mentioned as the last and unsuccessful commander of the CSS *Albemarle* in 1864. Yet between these events—and before and after them—he was the subject of no commentary. In many ways he was an example of military competence in waiting.

With no system for enforced retirement and with low retirement pay, the peacetime U.S. Navy, which Warley entered in 1840, was replete with old, often unable, and sometimes incompetent senior officers, whose retention effectively blocked promotion for the young. It took Warley fifteen years to make lieutenant. When the Confederate navy was formed in 1861, the senior lieutenant was James Cooke, with twenty-nine years of service. Warley was thirty-two places below him.

Thus for twenty years, Warley was a journeyman naval officer. Straight off the family farm in Pendleton, South Carolina, in 1840 he had little money, no naval mentor (until he married the daughter of Captain French Forrest in 1850), and no political connections (until first cousin William Porcher Miles was elected to Congress in 1856).

Warley hit his stride in 1861. He was competent, skilled, courageous, aggressive, and just senior enough to be in the right place, as a lieutenant, for the opportunities that opened up in the Confederate navy. Even as the number of seaworthy vessels decreased, he still earned commands—four in all and three of them ironclads. The money and most of the glory went to commanders of cruisers and blockade runners, but he was still among the elite of the Confederate navy. This South Carolinian was brave and aggressive and had definitely been around. This is his story.

I RESEARCHED WARLEY'S STORY off and on for forty years. Books about the Civil War, the U.S. and Confederate navies, and the service records of both navies provided the framework. The meat of the story came from ships' logs, books by Warley's contemporaries, letters, official reports, and travel vouchers. Some personal insights about Warley were found in records of his several courts-martial.

My search took me to the National Archives, the South Carolina Department of Archives and History, the U.S. Navy History and Heritage Command, the South Carolina Historical Society in Charleston, the Mississippi River from Fort Jackson to New Orleans, Charleston Harbor, the Roanoke River at Edward's Ferry and Plymouth, North Carolina, and naval museums across the South, as well as Boston, Newport, and St. Paul's Episcopal churchyard in Pendleton, South Carolina.

I thank my history-major bride of forty-three years, Priscilla, and Dr. William N. Still Jr. for assistance and encouragement. Thanks go as well to the people who assisted me at the many research institutions I visited, many of whom have retired by now.

PROMOTION *or the* BOTTOM OF THE RIVER

PROLOGUE

Christmas 1840

THE UNITED STATES SLOOP *Yorktown* plunged easily through the cool mid-Atlantic swells. The seventeen-year-old midshipman took the plunges less easily, but a little more comfortably than the day before. He was twelve days at sea and only seven months in the United States Navy.

Alexander Warley was formed up with the ship's company on this holy day, standing at attention—as well as he could when 120 feet of ship was in seaway—and regretting his distance from home. Home was Pendleton, South Carolina, almost twenty-one hundred nautical miles due west. Warley had eight siblings, so he was used to crowds, but he was not used to this crowd or this sort of Christmas. He was adapting.

After the captain's words were done, the festivities started. They began with the first of twelve lashes on the back of Seaman William Littlefield, who was being punished for neglect of duty. The captain had not mentioned the holiday.[1]

The Warleys had settled in the South Carolina lowcountry in the 1750s, acquiring more than two thousand acres in coastal Berkeley and Colleton Counties, around Charleston and Walterboro, where Alex Warley was born. Then, like so many in search of better land and healthier climate, the family moved upcountry to the Piedmont and settled in Pendleton. More temperate than the lowcountry and somewhat civilized by upcountry standards, this Anderson District town had attracted many planters from the coastal region, often on a seasonal basis. They had not yet pinned the cause of yellow fever on the mosquito, but they did know that the

Lieutenant Alexander Fraser Warley.
From Century Magazine, *Battles and
Leaders of the Civil War,* 1887–90.

marsh of the lowcountry killed white people in the summer time. While
the frontier nature of the upcountry was diminishing, life there was still
harsh.

Colonel Jacob Warley and his wife, Sophia, had established the Oaks
and were engaged in planting cotton and raising many children. Of the
twelve born to them, three of the first four children died in infancy, including a son named Alexander Fraser.[2] Twenty-two months after his birth, the
next son was born and given the same name. This Alexander, born in
Walterboro on July 29, 1823, was mostly raised in Pendleton, attended the
Pendleton Male Academy, and did well in literacy, penmanship, and basic
mathematics. He did have a temper.

When the colonel died in the summer of 1839, the family prevailed on
Senator John C. Calhoun for a naval appointment for their second son,
then almost seventeen. The navy was an unusual choice; the military was
not. Seven of the young man's uncles and cousins had been in the Continental Army or militia and had seen action during the Revolution. Four
had been taken prisoner at the fall of Charleston in 1780. The heritage was
to be continued.

1

FIRST TOUR

The Pacific aboard the USS *Yorktown*, 1840–1843

WITH AN APPOINTMENT as acting midshipman in hand and trepidation holding his stomach hostage, young Alexander Warley reported aboard the receiving ship in Norfolk, Virginia, on a cold February afternoon in 1840. A receiving ship was a miserable thing. No longer an operational vessel, it was old, sometimes dismasted and roofed over, used strictly as a barracks afloat for crews fitting out for the next man-of-war to be ready for sea. Indeed it was a jail of sorts for enlisted sailors, to prevent them from acting on any second thoughts about staying with the navy. Once aboard a receiving ship, they stayed. Officers had more flexibility, even if the younger ones had little means.

Most of the young midshipman's limited means were spent for uniforms. Besides the usual shirts, trousers, stockings, shoes, and underdrawers, he purchased uniform overcoats and short jackets, which displayed double rows of navy buttons and a buff colored anchor on each collar. He needed a full-dress cocked hat, which was expensive and had to be kept carefully, and a cap with anchor device for "undress" uniform. Not the least expensive items were the sword and the quadrant that were required of all youngsters entering the navy. The sword belt and decorative knot alone set him back twenty-nine dollars of his total four-hundred-dollar annual pay.[1]

With relief and trepidation, Midshipman Warley moved to the third-class sloop *Yorktown* on October 10, 1840, as it was fitting out for its Pacific deployment. Just two years old, the sloop was of the *Dale* class, designed as "economical cruisers" suited for distant stations for long periods. The *Yorktown* mounted sixteen carronades (thirty-two pounders) in peacetime and

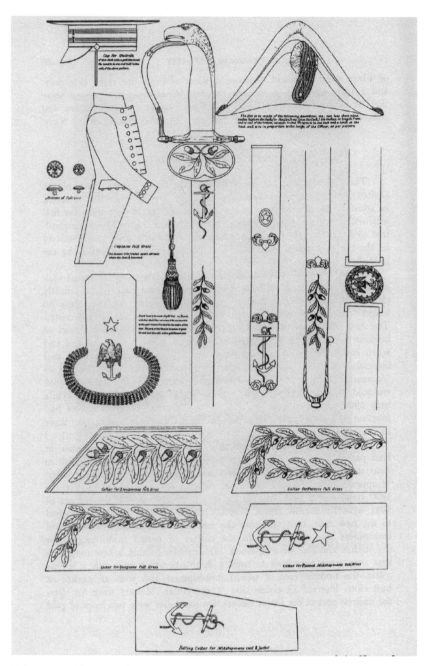

U.S. Navy uniforms and insignia in 1841. Warley purchased similar items when he entered the service a year earlier. From "Regulations for the Uniform and Dress of the Navy of the United States," 1841.

could ship two long guns if war seemed imminent.[2] The *Yorktown* was 118 feet between perpendiculars, had a 32-foot beam width, and its hold depth was 15 feet. Total displacement was 566 tons. As a smaller ship, it was a good vessel on which to begin a career. A junior man could not lose himself in a small ship, as he could on a ship of the line.

This Christmas the *Yorktown* was bound for the Pacific Squadron. It would be almost three years until the ship or its crew would return to the United States. Commander John H. Aulick had to mold his command into an effective sailing and fighting force to face the uncertainties of years and miles and foreign ports—as well as the changing conditions of the world, which changed more slowly in 1840 than today, but still faster than communications to deployed vessels. Making decisions based on incomplete information was, and is, a major burden for the military and is often a true test of officer material.

Beginning in 1815, the United States had established its modest global presence by developing five deployed squadrons. The first, in the Mediterranean, was followed by squadrons for Africa, Brazil (often including the West Indies), the Pacific, and the East Indies. Vessels in commission and not otherwise deployed formed the Home Squadron. Commanded by a captain carrying the title of commodore, these squadrons were actually area commands, not operational units. Each of the three to five vessels in a squadron generally cruised independently, meeting with the other vessels at predetermined locations. This squadron concept remained in use until the beginning of the Civil War.

Captain Aulick had a wardroom of three lieutenants, a surgeon, and a purser. There were eight midshipmen in steerage, four of whom were passed midshipmen—a grade senior to acting midshipmen—and therefore somewhat useful. The four acting midshipmen were considered to have varying "potential." Steerage was the bunk room for these "reefers" and gave them more creature comforts than the crew had. The reefers' hammocks had more bedding and were stowed for them by cot boys. There was a tin-basin washstand, filled by a deck bucket, and each lad could claim his own camp stool and locker, small though it was.

Generally the first lieutenant did not stand a watch, but on a sloop, with only three lieutenants, "number one" spent some regular time on deck along with the passed "mids." In addition to "formal studies," mids stood watch under instruction, and were in the tops and at various points around deck when all hands were called. They mustered the watch at night, took "noon shots" with their quadrants, kept journals of the cruise, and were

The ship of war *Yorktown*. From William Brady, *The Kedge-Anchor,* 1847.

boat officers in port. Each also had one or more guns to command at action quarters. The surgeon and purser—and on larger vessels the chaplain and officers of the marines—stood no regular watches and were therefore collectively termed "idlers."

Warley had fallen in with a captain who had earned the reputation for being a martinet.[3] Aulick was singularly harsh on his midshipmen, having told one, "Sir, when I get a midshipman on board my ship I never let him go ashore until I know something about him." This form of leadership often fosters unusually strong bonds among the junior officers (united against the captain). Aulick had the reputation for doing that too.

From the East Coast of the United States down to Rio, the new ship's company drilled at the guns, ran to general quarters, worked the rigging, and repeated it all again and again. Running to general quarters—battle stations—was not easy. Every bulkhead had to be knocked down, so that no artificial barrier to movement remained. On larger vessels, guns were mounted in the cabins of the captain and even the commodore. Sailors' mess chests were tumbled down into the hold; chains were slung from the rigging; and hospital cots were dragged from the sail room and piled at hand. Cannonballs were brought up and stored between the guns; shot plugs were slung overhead within easy reach; and the solid masses of wads, big as Dutch cheeses, were braced to the cheeks of the gun carriages. At the guns the first and second loaders stood ready to receive their supplies. Powder monkeys obtained the cartridges through a small arm hole in a wooden screen at the entrance to the magazine at the berth deck. To protect the cartridges from fire or red-hot shot, the lads learned to wrap them in their jackets and scramble to their respective guns. When a ship was ready for battle within five minutes or at the satisfaction of the captain (perhaps four minutes), the ship's company practiced running out the guns, simulating firing, or actually firing, them. At the sound of the boarding rattle, the company rushed from the guns, seized cutlasses and pikes, and flailed at the imaginary enemy. Then they went back to the guns. At the call of "fire in the foretop," they manned the pumps. The crew learned repeatedly the meaning of readiness and discipline. Littlefield was not the only man flogged on this leg of the journey. Harsh treatment in the first months of the cruise established the standards of behavior desired to maintain proper discipline.

Warley learned this routine time and time again. He also learned the nuances of battle. As Herman Melville advised in *White-Jacket* (1850), Warley was told, "Wear the older, looser uniform (when you have one)—it affords more freedom of movement and is not so expensive if cut away from your wounds." He was also told that officers, who had the option, should fight in silk stockings, as silk is easier to pick from a leg wound than cotton, which sticks and works into the flesh.

As January became unseasonably hot, King Neptune and his court came "over the side" and extracted bounty from the ship as it crossed his line. The time-honored ceremony at crossing the equator had begun, and the king of all that is under the sea desired the beards of all "pollywogs," those aboard who had never before crossed the line. To extract their beards, the king brought the royal barber and his assistants, who removed the supposed hairs along with the lather of coal dust and soapy water, with just a taste of tar. The victim was then tipped backward from the chair into a sail basin of water and washed by more assistants. The "shellback" veterans hooted and enjoyed the fun, especially at the expense of the youngsters. Warley survived, as almost all do.

The first stop for a ship bound to anywhere except the Mediterranean was Rio de Janeiro, the port that often provided the first foreign experience for anyone new to the navy. Rio was center point of the Brazil Squadron and exotic—at least by American standards.

The *Yorktown* made its approach around Cape Frio on January 24, 1841,[4] and swung north between the forts and into the harbor. Ships often approached Rio under full sail, swinging into the wind and letting go with a grand flourish. As the first stop with a fresh crew, it was a professional test, in full view of all ships anchored in the harbor. If even the seventy-four-gun ships of the line could hazard this maneuver with their flag officers breathing raspily over the captain's shoulder, a mere commander had better perform. Aulick performed.

The boat of the captain of the port was the official welcome. The official boat was rowed by "real Africans," using long sweeps, a manner peculiar to Brazilian craft, in which oarsmen stood at the start of the pull, putting their whole weight on the sweep and sinking into their seats at the end of the stroke. The boat was long and covered aft with an awning, shading the assistant to the captain that a mere sloop would rate.[5]

Most local craft in the harbor featured boomless, rectangular lug sails. The white of the sails and the houses and the lush green of the surrounding mountains with Sugarloaf as the centerpiece, gave this landlocked anchorage a breathtaking vertical beauty.

This beauty was not lost on the seventeen-year-old Warley, but not much was gained by the midshipmen. The officers were given a little shore leave during the twelve days the ship was in port, but the men were generally all stuck aboard, except for the boat crews who rowed the officers ashore or went to the Rat Island depot that the United States maintained for provisioning its ships. Water and ship's stores had to be topped off.

All hands, officers included, were allowed one "ration" per day. An officer had the option of stopping his rations, taking instead six dollars per month to be used for his own mess fund. To create such a fund, it helped to have a nest egg from one's prior existence. Warley's family was modestly prosperous but not overly comfortable. It did not supplement his present income. All his life he budgeted his expenditures carefully or paid the consequences.

The rations for the men were specified by regulation: one and a half pounds of biscuit a day, one pint of beans three times per week, three-quarters of a pound of flour, two ounces of raisins, a quarter pound of butter, a quarter pound of cheese, a gill of molasses, a gill of vinegar, and a half pint of rice all twice a week. (A gill is one-fourth of a pint.) There was an alternating daily allowance of tea, coffee, or cocoa. A pound and a half of beef was distributed four times a week; a quarter pound of pork was provided on each of the other three days; and one half gill of grog was served each breakfast and dinner.[6] Some chroniclers say this alcohol ration made the water drinkable. It also served to dull the senses.

Once a ship was in the fine anchorage of Rio, the monotony of diet and company was relieved somewhat by the swarm of native bumboats selling various provisions. Their visits also relieved the crew of any spare money.

The quarterdeck, used for ceremonies involving visitations and officer transit, was in those days on the starboard side with all other access to the ship at anchor being on the port, in those days called "larboard." Enlisted men's movements, official provisioning, and traders' boarding from the bumboats all took place on the larboard side. After inspection by some authorities, including medical officers if available, the bumboats did a thriving business with the crew in local fruits, soft bread, and other foods and trinkets.

The published daily ration, which did not specify the condition of the foodstuffs themselves, did not include fruits and vegetables. The bumboats in Rio helped to correct this deficiency if only temporarily. Bananas, in their own wrappers (to the amazement of the new men), accompanied guavas, coconuts, and oranges. In addition to soft bread, there were also boiled eggs and other local delicacies. Men allowed shore leave could obtain these foods ashore, but most of the crew could buy them only from the bumboats. Most of these perishable items lasted no more than two days out of port. Then it was back to the published menu, whose palatability could be enhanced or hindered according to the talents of the various mess cooks.

As a major crossroads harbor, Rio was a gathering place for world navies, and all visitors observed the formalities of their own government, their neighbors, and their hosts. This called for a lot of saluting, considerable decorating, and much holidaying, especially in observance of all the saints claimed by the Brazilian government and the Catholic Church. All this "catching up" of holidays may be connected to their almost total non-observance while a ship was at sea.

The *Yorktown* weighed anchor on February 5 and stood out to sea, its stores and tanks filled and most of the pockets of its crew empty. Young Warley had not made it ashore and was now nervously anticipating Cape Horn.

One month later, the passage of the cape was begun. The combination of high (and usually contrary) winds, incredibly rough seas, and cold temperatures made rounding Cape Horn a harrowing event. Severe weather changes were commonplace. It became cold. Heating in a wooden sailing ship was a challenge. Because of the threat of fire, generally only the galley fires were allowed, and these were constantly supervised. A young man in steerage could bring a heated solid shot in a bucket of sand back to his quarters for whatever comfort it might provide. Returning from a watch on deck, he could recover a little by sticking his bare feet in the sand, being careful not to touch the red-hot shot itself.

For three days, the *Yorktown* stood against the seas at the bottom of the world, beginning far south—almost to the peninsula of Antarctica known as Palmer's Land—to try to gain some freeway (that is, "headway"). Forty-foot seas in a sloop precluded cooking, almost precluded eating and any other manner of creature comfort. On the seventh, Aulick's command broke through the invisible barrier that finally allowed a northerly heading without the danger of the ship being thrown on South America's lee shore. Two weeks later they arrived in Valparaiso, Chile.

A "good navy town," Valparaiso sits below a plain that offers a magnificent view of the harbor and approaches to it. From this plain almost the entire population of the city witnessed the 1814 battle in which the HMS *Phoebe* and *Cherub* took David Porter in the USS *Essex*. From this point too, individuals witnessed the arrival of ships and plotted the extraction of money from their crews. As a major liberty port, Valparaiso, whose name may be translated as "vale of paradise," was considered as such only by those who had experienced little in the way of comparison. The city was rough. For many it was rough fun, and they wanted to stay. As an assistance to those ships that could not recover their crews, the local police, the "Vigilantes," could be hired for bounty to retrieve those last few sailors who did not want to return to their ships. As their time and money ran out, late returners hoping to avoid the additional manhandling that the Vigilantes would inflict, would attempt to break through the Chilean cordon around the port and turn themselves in to the relatively gentle justice of captain's mast, nonjudicial punishment. U.S. vessels might assist men in their return to avoid paying the bounty whenever possible. When a bounty had to be paid, however, it was usually deducted from the pay of the culprit. A week in Chile was sufficient for the new mids, who were still "unknown enough" to the captain and were held aboard.

The ship continued up the South American continent to Callao, Peru, and experienced ten days of increasing warmth. The *Yorktown* arrived at this seaport city, nine miles from the Peruvian capital of Lima, on April 6. It never seems to rain in coastal Peru. Instead a dense mist—a dew of the heaviest type—wets land and sea all night as a solid rain would.[7]

Night-watch standers hated it. Young Warley tired of it thoroughly as he endured it into late May. A train provided transport between Callao and Lima, which was a beautifully laid-out city, rich in the Spanish heritage of raiding and colonization. In the few years that followed, it was also the center of impromptu changes of government. Visiting warships often arrived during a revolution and carefully avoided taking sides.

On May 26, 1841, Aulick took his command 480 miles north to Paita, Peru, an excellent harbor with a fine climate. Though the harbor led to a lush and fertile valley, there was no fresh water within ten miles of the town. The road leading to the nearest river was littered with the bones of dead donkeys. Four days later, the *Yorktown* was back at sea, bound for fairer lands.

For more than seventy years, the Society Islands had held a special place in the hearts and minds of seafarers. Drawn by stories of the friendliness, hospitality, and generosity of the Tahitians, most especially the female Tahitians, visitors were taken first by the sheer physical beauty of the great, green, sweeping vista of Tahiti. Rising more than seven thousand feet from the sea, the mountains of the larger Tahiti Nui section were complemented by Mount Ronui on Tahiti Iti, the peninsula that formed the handle of the hand-mirror-shaped island. Thousand-foot waterfalls accented the tropical lushness. The natives—though still a friendly, open people—had been somewhat calloused by repeated visits of European ships. They were more mercenary than in the days of Captain James Cook's visits in 1769 and 1773—which was noted by the crew of HMS *Bounty* in 1789. The half century of imported illness that followed Cook's visits had depleted the island group's prediscovery population of an estimated fifty thousand by 75 percent.[8] However, when the *Yorktown* entered Papeete Bay on the island's northern shore on July 6, the crew was not disappointed. It was a time of stress between the forces of fraternity and the restraints of discipline. When the ship departed eighteen days later, it was short six hands, and five were flogged for not making the departure in "a proper manner."

After three weeks at sea, one week in the Bay of Islands, on the North Island of New Zealand, the *Yorktown* returned to Tahiti, this time to Matavia Bay, just six miles from the original port of call. There is no record that the six deserters were found. On this second visit some of the men went ashore through the surf to Venus Point, where Captain Cook had established an observatory to view the transit of the planet Venus. Then the *Yorktown* sailed north 2,730 miles to the Sandwich Islands (now Hawaii), for an anchorage off the settlement of Lahaina on Maui's west coast. At the time Hawaii was short of good harbors, which were constructed later. The Lahaina Roads anchorage was favorable in most prevailing winds. This location near a town of friendly natives not only attracted navy vessels but became a major center for Pacific whaling fleets during the 1840s. The *Yorktown* spent only four days of provisioning in Hawaii before heading east to California, averaging five knots on the way to Monterey.

The ship spent the next month beating down the coast of new and old Mexico (northern and southern California). At Christmas 1841 Warley was still at sea, again with no ceremonies, just observing more ocean and anticipating crossing the equator for the third time in his short life. No ceremonies were held there either as the entire crew was shellbacks. No number of maps (and there were a small number of them) in the Pendleton Male Academy would have prepared him for this experience. No sea state is understood until felt, and no harbor is experienced until smelled. Warley may have been weighing his general good fortune and balancing that with memories of home as he found himself in the water-short harbor of Paita, Peru, once more.

On the birthday of George Washington, the *Yorktown* exchanged salutes with the other vessels at Valparaiso, where the *Yorktown* spent the next three weeks, provisioning once again. The ship had arrived at Valparaiso with only 56 gallons of whiskey remaining. These were supplemented with 1,000 gallons more, plus 13,000 gallons of water and 13,000 pounds of bread. In these tropical waters in these summer months (it was February), the men of *Yorktown* consumed 130 to 150 gallons of water per day. Making time at sea (and the water) a bit more palatable, were the 2 gallons of spirits, watered down and issued each morning and eve.

Usually punishment was awarded in port. On March 16 the *Yorktown* log reported, "Corporal Howard was disrated and awarded twelve lashes with a piece of 9 thread ratline stuff by order of and in the presence of the captain for insubordinate language and conduct." Meanwhile events many miles away conspired to make life a little easier for the crew. Commander John Aulick was promoted to captain. It would take some time for a change of command to alter things locally, but he had now outgrown his sloop command and there was a chance that someone less stringent might replace him. It was true then as now, that within two or three years, the navy would see to it a sailor and his superior would part. While such personnel changes are regrettable in some instances, they provide great hope for many others. This hope is sometimes dashed.

The *Yorktown* spent the spring of 1842 cruising the west coast of South America: Valparaiso to Callao to Pisco to Callao. Aulick, while perhaps anticipating his departure, did not become overly good natured. He might have been allowing some time ashore, but there was a price to pay for time poorly spent there. Several men felt the lash in the harbor of Callao for quarreling and intoxication. "Twelve lashes with nine thread stuff."

In Callao on May 31, Captain Aulick was relieved by Commander John S. Nichols, and Midshipman Warley was transferred to the schooner *Shark* (under Lieutenant Commanding H. Eagle). Transfer from ship to ship was part of a midshipman's education, to assure that he saw different ships and different processes. Warley spent three months aboard the *Shark* and then transferred directly to the sloop *Cyane* (under Commander C. K. Stribling) for another three months of "temporary additional duty." Both these skippers wrote well of him in their recommendation letters, which passed for fitness reports at that time, as did Commander Nichols at the end of the cruise. These letters, together with a written request for a warrant, were submitted by Warley to remove the "acting" from his midshipman status. He sent these to the secretary of the navy on his return to Norfolk in August 1843, but his warrant had already been approved in July 1842. Apparently two years in the probationary grade were enough. Warley retained copies of these letters, in a time-honored act of prudence, and they later proved valuable.

The schooner *Shark* was a much older, much smaller ship than the modestly sized sloop *Yorktown*. Warley found himself aboard a twenty-one-year-old topsail schooner of eighty-six feet in length. The *Shark's* twelve guns were not that many more than the number carried by the China-trade clippers that it resembled. Less comfortable and less formal than the *Yorktown,* the *Shark* was a good command for a lieutenant and good notch in young Warley's education.

A schooner was a serious turn of education after Warley's square-rigged beginning. Meant to be fast, with the ability to "get up and go" in a hurry, the *Shark* carried a lot of sail, a disproportionate amount on the foremast. The forecourse, or foresail, was suspended by a gaff above but had no boom, thus allowing it to overlap the mainsail and also lessening the weight aloft forward. The topsail rigging was also designed for quick lowering. All that canvas—especially when wet, as it would be in heavy weather—and the spars topside created too much weight aloft. This increased the uncomfortable tendency of schooners, when hard driven, to run the bow under.[9]

The schooner *Shark*. From William Brady, *The Kedge-Anchor*, 1847.

His three months on *Shark* gave Midshipman Warley an appreciation of schooners and their distinctive characteristics, but he never spent time on one again.

On August 29, 1842, at the end of his tour aboard the *Shark*, the young Carolinian hauled his belongings on the jolly boat (the smallest boat a ship carried) across the Callao harbor to the USS *Cyane*, a step up from his previous experience and into a new level of excitement. He also found friends aboard the *Cyane* who almost proved his undoing.

The first *Cyane* had been captured from the British in 1815. This original had been broken up in 1836, but under a system[10] where Congress had allotted funds only for repair and not for new construction, the *Cyane* had been "administratively rebuilt" from the original at the Charlestown Navy Yard about 1837. It was actually new, a "second class ship sloop" and—at 132 feet in length with a 34-foot beam—a bit larger than the *Yorktown*, rating two more guns (eighteen) with capabilities of twenty-two.

The Royal Navy's Pacific Fleet under Rear Admiral Richard Thomas had shared the Callao anchorage with the American squadron. Commodore Thomas ap Catesby Jones of the U.S. Navy, a savvy old Virginian, was concerned about the future of California and sat aboard the frigate *United States* eyeing the British. Having been a gunboat commander during the Battle of New Orleans in 1815, Jones still carried a British musket ball in his left shoulder and a genuine distrust of its makers in his mind.

Jones had a collection of newspapers and letters that strongly put forth the possibility of war with Mexico. The most recent correspondence from the U.S. ambassador to Mexico—letters by then two months old— included a copy of a letter from José María de Bocanegra, the Mexican minister of foreign relations, to U.S. Secretary of State Daniel Webster, which could be interpreted as a conditional declaration of war. Jones interpreted it in this manner. As Mexico had never formally recognized the independence of Texas, relations between the United States and Mexico were perpetually testy, and the language of Bocanegra's letter went beyond the accepted bounds of diplomacy.[11] There was also a continued possibility that Mexico might settle its long-term debts to the British by ceding them California. England had designs on the entire upper coast of North America and was in dispute with the United States over northern boundaries of the Oregon Territory. The United States in fact had no diplomatic representation north of Mazatlán while the British maintained a consulate in Monterey.

Jones's most recent instructions, which he had carried from home, were nine months old, and he faced a six-month gap between a request for direction and a reply from Washington. Too much could be lost by operating by the book, and naval officers on distant stations were not placed there because of their lack of initiative. Knowing that his duty was to save something of great value (California)—yet not put his nation at war—placed Commodore Jones in the position of looking for a sign.

When Admiral Thomas took his squadron out of Callao under sealed orders, Jones had his sign and had to move. By now, almost certain that Thomas was headed to Panama to pick up troops and head north to take over California, Jones took his squadron—the *United States,* the *Cyane,* and the *Dale*—south to Lima to consult with the U.S. consul there. Then they returned to Callao to prepare for conflict.

In a conference with his captains, Jones outlined the situation and received their concurrence in the action to secure California. He described his situation in a letter to Navy Secretary Abel P. Upshur, saying that he was alone in the Pacific contending with a superior British squadron, which appeared to have serious intentions of occupying California. He also expressed concerns about a French fleet that had just occupied the

Marquesas, some nine hundred miles northwest of Tahiti. He reiterated that he was without instructions, and "all that I can promise is a faithful and zealous application of my best abilities to promote and sustain the honor and welfare of our country."[12] Dispatching the *Dale* to Panama to start this correspondence on its way, Jones headed north on September 8 to Monterey with the *United States,* the *Cyane,* and Mr. Warley.

Young Warley had experienced his gun drills aboard *Yorktown,* and he now had his own gun and crew. With his new ordnance and team aboard the *Cyane,* they ran out the guns, fired at barrel targets thrown over the side, and put an edge to their cutlasses.

On October 18, 1842, just south of Monterey, California, Captain Stribling of the *Cyane* read to his crew the general order of the commodore. It stated that, while they might fight Mexican soldiers, they must protect the civilians. It went on to lay out strict discipline and called on the honor and good behavior of the men of both ships. Two days later the small American squadron rounded Point Pinos into Monterey Bay, cleared for action and flying British colors. The *United States* anchored in seven fathoms of water and swung between bow anchor and kedge to bring the port guns to bear on town and fort. At this time they flew a flag of truce and inquired about the brig *Fama* of Boston, recently in from Honolulu (generally a clearinghouse for news in the Pacific). The brig's captain reported rumors in the Sandwich Islands that war between Mexico and the United States was imminent and that Mexico was said to have ceded California to Britain.[13] Even in the absence of the Royal Navy, Jones was apprehensive about the possibility of their sudden appearance and concluded that possession of the dilapidated fort would place him in a more solid position.

At four in the afternoon, Jones sent a demand for surrender of the fort, all military posts, troops, arms, and munitions within eighteen hours. Rapid conferences ashore between governor and commandant confirmed that the fort contained a garrison of twenty-nine military and twenty-five untrained individuals, all with a similar lack of fighting capability. There were eleven cannon, whose carriages were at best precarious, and a small supply of powder. The governor had hoped for at least an honorable show of resistance, but he faced reality and sent a boat to the flagship late that evening to negotiate. Jones had already retired, but he rose again for the conference and accepted the surrender of the fort and town and all forces in Monterey.

The only questions from the Californians were raised by local merchant Thomas O. Larkin, serving as translator. He alone seemed curious about why the ships had suddenly descended on Monterey and if war had been declared. Jones said that a de facto war had been declared by Mexico, citing the foreign minister's message. Larkin said that he was in possession of newspapers ashore that said as late as August (three months more recent than the commodore's information) that relations between the nations were peaceful.

At 7:30 on the morning of October 21, the surrender papers were signed and Jones went ashore, soon finding unopened newspapers from August confirming that relations between the United States and Mexico were cordial and that rumors of Britain's control of California were completely false. The American commander had now to walk a precarious line in California. His standing back in Washington was much more uncertain.

After conferring with his captains, Jones wrote to the California authorities explaining that the difficulties precipitating the capture had been previously corrected and returned all surrendered entities with extreme apologies. It had been an interesting capture; the only ordnance expended had been that used in salutes exchanged between ships and fort after the surrender. The fleet sent ninety-five pounds of powder to the fort to replace what they had used. American control of California had lasted under two days.

While the government in Mexico City showed considerable affront at the proceedings, the locals took it in good grace and displayed their best hospitality toward the conquerors/visitors. The midshipmen in particular enjoyed themselves, being invited to social events by the senoritas. Many a young man learned to dance at the formal and informal dances hosted in private homes in town. This phase in his education was delayed for Warley, however, as the *Cyane* was sent north to Santa Barbara on October 23.

He returned to Monterey on November 12 and had at least a week and a half to acquaint himself socially ashore until, on the twenty-first, he saw his old home, the *Yorktown*, anchor in the bay. The next afternoon he transferred back aboard that ship, bringing with him sea stories that his shipmates could not yet match, as bloodless and calm as they were.

The *Yorktown* went south for the winter and spent the next two months in Mazatlán, a favorite wintering port for the Pacific Squadron. Wintering in Mazatlán is still a favorite of North Americans. On a latitude comparable to Hawaii, Mazatlán has winter temperatures in the sixties. Entering the harbor between the huge guardian rocks of El Faro to port and Stone Island to starboard, the first-time visitor is not expecting the great sweep of almost eight miles of curving harbor. The town of Mazatlán, spread out on the peninsula to the left had been occupied for two hundred years when the *Yorktown* visited but organized for only twenty.

Apparently some of the crew enjoyed their visit too much. As the squadron was preparing for sea on February 13, 1843, the *Yorktown*'s log read: "Results of late court martial aboard Yorktown were read and at 9:00 the commodore made signal #1049, crossed top gallant and royal yards and rove the gear. At 9:15 signal 894, at 9:45 #316, at 10:00 we fired a gun and squadron hoisted a Yellow Flag at the fore, called all hands to witness punishment. Three men to receive 100 lashes, four men, 50 lashes. One half the number applied and sent to the flagship for remainder." On the next day the captain addressed the crew on the subject of abolishing spirits. There may well have been a connection between these events, and not just because the squadron may have received word from home that the spirit ration for midshipmen had been done away with. According to the Articles of War, one hundred lashes could be awarded for drunkenness or mutinous conduct, but this punishment was often mitigated to fifty. The penalty for desertion was fifty lashes, and that for mutinous conduct with respect to a superior officer was set at eighty lashes. The actual award of one hundred lashes was often approaching the penalty of death.[14]

The journey home seemed to take longer than any other phase of the trip. After two months underway, the *Yorktown* reached Valparaiso on April 13 and remained until May 3. Parts of the ship needed caulking, and it always required painting. English and French ships were in harbor, and this also called for the requisite formalities, including a twenty-one-gun salute for the birthday of Louis Philippe on May first.

Heading south, the crew had their first experience of snow and hail on May 22 and knew they were in for another uncomfortable winter passage of Cape Horn. Early June produced five straight days of snow. Snow was heavy and had to be removed. Each gun captain was responsible for keeping his station clean. Old brooms and "squilgees," leather hoelike devices used to dry the water from washed decks, were employed to drag the snow over the side. They hit the southernmost point of transit on the fourth. On June 10 the officer of the deck recorded that the temperature exceeded 50 degrees for the first time since May 13.

The author Herman Melville was on the frigate *United States* rounding Cape Horn in the winter of 1843, when it was becalmed for forty-eight hours in deadly cold. Lacking even hot sand to warm their feet, the crew suffered terribly until, on the second day, they heard the bosun's pipe and sound attention. The bosun, on order of the captain, called, "D'ye hear there, fore and aft! All hands—skylark!" At this word—given and taken to mean "play"—discipline went by the board; officers and petty officers stood back; and general pandemonium ensued until things got out of hand, someone got hurt and order was restored. But for a couple of hours, tension was relieved and the activity of the crew warmed them all.

Not everyone survived the ordeal of cold aboard *Yorktown*. Armorer John White's body was committed to the deep on June 13, 1843.

By June 19 the sloop was beating up for the harbor at Rio de Janeiro, and the next day they hailed a British man-of-war departing that busy place. On June 21 they entered the harbor at Rio, and this time the midshipmen could go ashore. Once anchored, however, there were formalities, including a twenty-one-gun salute to the Brazilian flag, which was answered by the same salute from Fort Villaganound, and then thirteen minute guns, slow-paced firing as a memorial to Commodore Isaac Hull of the U.S. Navy.

Provisions were loaded for the remaining six weeks to home. Taken on board in the course of one day were: two thousand pounds of bread, thirteen barrels of whiskey, nine barrels of beef, seven barrels of pork, one barrel of butter, four boxes of cheese, three barrels of flour, four boxes of raisins, one barrel of molasses, one case of vinegar, two and a half bags of beans, one and a half bags of rice, two boxes of candles, one box of shoes, two boxes of tobacco, one box of tea, one tank of water, two hundred fifty feet of lumber, and fifteen gallons of sperm oil. The next day they loaded five hundred sticks of wood, a boatload of sand, five gallons of spirits of turpentine, five gallons of paint oil, two thousand pump tacks, five gallons of tar, three kegs of white lead, and paint brushes. After two days of limited liberty, they were underway on June 27 for the navy yard at New York, where they arrived on August 6.

Waiting mail told young Warley that he was indeed warranted as a full midshipman and had earned three months leave for his three-year departure. He headed for Pendleton, where he found that only a little more than two months had been granted him. He was sent orders in late October, just two days after formally acknowledging his warrant. The youngster's next departure point was Philadelphia, his vehicle the frigate *Raritan*.

SECOND TOUR

Three Ships and the Naval Academy, 1843–1846

THE *RARITAN* was a brand new forty-four-gun frigate, in a manner of speaking. Just launched in mid-1843, it had been under construction for twenty-two years on the ways (inclined structures on which ships are built) in Philadelphia. When funding was slow, so was construction, and Congress had not seen the need for the expensive completion of the four "new" 44s it had authorized in 1819. In fact only the *Potomac* was hurried through to completion in 1822. The others were launched over the period of 1842–55.[1]

The *Raritan* was placed in commission by Captain Francis A. Gregory on November 15, 1843, and set to sea on December 2, arriving off Sandy Hook at New York a week later. Experiencing sickness in the crew, Gregory traded men with the Brooklyn Navy Yard and the receiving ship *North Carolina* to bolster his complement. Six of the transfers demonstrated their discontent and desperation on Christmas Day by attempting to swim the unbelievably cold waters of the harbor to freedom. They were "retrieved."

The frigate sat at New York until mid-February, when it took on passengers for Rio. It also completed the acquisition of supplies, including 24 belaying pins, 18 kegs of pickles, and 175½ barrels of whiskey. In return it set ashore Midshipman Warley, who was now "waiting orders."

Less than a week later, on February 21, 1844, the Navy Department sent him to Norfolk to meet the frigate *Constitution*. He carried with him a letter of good character from Captain Gregory, which later proved but a feeble defense against the personality of his new commander, Captain "Roaring John" Percival.

Also referred to as "Mad Jack," Percival had begun his years at sea in 1797, when he was unwillingly impressed into the Royal Navy for two years aboard HMS *Victory*. After distinguishing himself in the War of 1812 against the British, he later sailed extensively in the Pacific. Irascible and unpredictable, he was a seaman first and a fighter as a close second.[2] Percival was taking Old Ironsides to China, with a stop at Rio on the way. With him and his officers were 381 men, of whom only 169 were Americans. Navy crews were normally cosmopolitan. The crew of the *Constitution* included 50 Irishmen, 43 Englishmen, and representatives from most traditional seafaring European nations, including 19 Swedes.[3] None of Percival's thirty fellow officers was foreign. Warley found himself in the relative obscurity of steerage aboard the nation's most famous warship.

It was to be a cruise of three years. Backtracking first to New York, the *Constitution* took on seventeen passengers, notably including the U.S. minister to Brazil, Henry A. Wise, his family, secretary, and servants. Two naval lieutenants and a marine lieutenant, heading for ships in Rio, also embarked. On May 29, 1844, the old frigate shook loose its sails at Sandy Hook and headed to the southeast. All transits in and out of the harbors had been conducted with the aid of steam tugboats, a point of some interest to the second-cruise midshipman.

In two weeks they raised the Azores, and using the occasionally active volcano on the island of Saint Mary's as a reference, they wrestled with contrary winds for four days before dropping the hook into eighty fathoms of water off the port of Fagal. Three and a half days were spent in back-and-forth visitations and parties, often involving Minister Wise, the American consul, ship's officers, and a few midshipmen (perhaps including Warley) for window dressing and social add-ons. Three days later, many of the same cast of players replayed these activities on the island of Madeira. They did so again on July 4 in Tenerife, in the Canaries.

Having spent almost every noon on the quarterdeck, quadrant rolling with the swells, determining the sun line, and the consensus (usually led by the captain or sailing master) about the exact moment of "noon." "Make it so, Mr. Paine." would be Captain Percival's official declaration for the log. Warley was not surprised this time by the appearance in the middle of the ocean near the equator, by the god Zeus, in this case a servant of the great Neptune. Appearing on a line from over the side, Zeus delivered a letter to

Captain Percival demanding tribute, once more in the form of beards (un-necessary in the southern latitudes, but available for distribution to his followers in the north). He was to appear the next day and hoped for a favorable answer. The captain provided it.

Perhaps because the Wises were aboard, or perhaps because the ship was the *Constitution,* or just because of Percival, Neptune arrived in glory, in a wagon with a retinue of a dozen well-costumed sailors. After greeting the officers and guests and receiving two flagons of wine, Neptune estab-lished his barbershop and treated the uninitiated for almost three hours.[4] During it all shellback Warley watched with the pleasure of one who had had the experience and needed never to face it again.

Obscurity came to a glorious termination when Warley looked out across the beautiful anchorage at Rio and spied the sloop *Cyane,* heading home from its three years on the other side of the world with old friends aboard. It had been a little less than two years since Warley had been aboard the *Cyane,* when he and his mates had "taken" Monterey and then enjoyed its social life. As coincidence would have it, just four years had passed since Captain Percival had brought the *Cyane* back from the Medi-terranean. The captain had no social contacts aboard the sloop, but the midshipman did.

On August 12 Warley was invited to the *Cyane* for an evening visit with his friends. Drinks were included, and the young South Carolinian may have been sabotaged. Whether induced or self-induced, his intake exceeded his tolerance, and he arrived back aboard the *Constitution* in pitiful con-dition. Shedding his clothes, he appeared stark naked on the gun deck in view of much of the crew. (It would be hard to hide from anyone for long onboard a man-of-war.) First Lieutenant Amasa Paine told Warley to go be bed and be quiet.[5] Lieutenant James Alden followed along and tried to enforce the rules of sobriety. Midshipman Warley was beyond reason, and his steerage messmates were recruited to help. For his efforts Passed Mid-shipman Knapp was challenged to a duel by Warley and threatened with ambush if he would not accept the challenge. Knapp shouldered this bar-rage with general resignation as part of the problem of dealing with a drunk. Warley was finally settled down, having provided sufficient enter-tainment and fuss for the evening.

Of course that was not the end of it. Charges were assembled even as Warley's hangover was dissipating. Three days after the event, in an attempt at damage control, Warley wrote an extremely proper and contrite letter of apology to Captain Percival. On August 17 Captain Francis Gregory convened the court-martial of his former junior officer aboard the *Raritan*. Assisting Gregory were Captain P. Y. Voorhees, Commanders George Hollins and William Newman, Lieutenant Commanding T. D. Shaw, and Lieutenants R. S. Browning and B. Shepard. Chaplain John Robb, as judge advocate, handled the legalities.

Charges preferred by Captain Percival included drunkenness, scandalous conduct leading to the destruction of good morals, disobedience of orders, and use of provoking or reproachful words to another person in the navy. While the bringing of so many charges may have the appearance of "piling on," such a collection of charges probably did and still does commonly lead from the basic charge of "drunk and disorderly."

Following the reading of the charges, which had been prepared two days prior, Captain Percival showed no less tenacity against his junior officer than he had against the British in 1812. He added the charge of mutiny and mutinous conduct for Warley's challenge of Passed Midshipman Knapp. Warley, having no defense, attempted none and submitted a letter of explanation of the reunion with old shipmates: "In that joyous overflow of good feeling which everyone can appreciate but none ascribe, I drank—drank to our meeting—to their homeward passage—to their meeting with those loved at home and before I was aware of it had drunk too much." He referred to his letter of apology to Percival and included complimentary letters of recommendation from previous commanding officers, including one from the *Cyane* eighteen months earlier. On the reverse of his letter he added the fact that he and Passed Midshipman Knapp had always been the best of friends.

Taking note of Percival's objection that Warley's letter was not legal evidence, the court was cleared and in short order found the midshipman guilty on all the original charges, plus mutinous conduct, but not mutiny. He was sentenced to be dismissed from the United States Navy. In a rare move, possibly sparked by Captain Gregory's experience with the young man, the unanimous addendum to the sentence by the court read: "The court, upon mature reflection, and deliberation has leave respectfully to recommend the accused to mercy, on account of his previous good character, as appears from the testimonials presented by him upon his trial, and hereunto appended." It was up to the Department of the Navy to decide which course to take, and Warley would have to wait for that decision.

It took a month for Warley and the documents to reach Washington, where he waited until the court-martial results arrived in the Navy Department. The packet hit the desk of Navy Secretary John Young Mason on

October 4 and included the favorable endorsement of Squadron Commodore Daniel Turner. The secretary immediately endorsed it favorably, and the next day, President John Tyler wrote in his own hand, "The sentence is approved, but in consideration of the fair and heretofore unexceptionable character of Mr. Warley, the sentence is remitted."

In the strange and wonderful workings of the navy, Warley was then granted three months leave, only to have it cancelled a week and a half later, when he was sent orders to report to the steamer *Colonel Harney* in Philadelphia. Steam power was coming to the navy, and this assignment was Warley's first association with it.

At first glimpse assignment to the *Colonel Harney* might have appeared a punishment for a young man lucky to have his job at all. The steamer was named after William S. Harney, who had distinguished himself in the Seminole War of 1840. Harney was still serving and was later brevetted a brigadier in the Mexican War. His namesake was a 133-foot side-wheel steamer that had been built for the army in 1840 and had just been transferred to the navy,[6] causing Warley to be a plank owner, a member of the commissioning crew for a new ship—at least for navy purposes.

On reflection and perhaps from experience, the young man might have realized that duty for a twenty-two-year-old on an early steamer—with a lieutenant commanding and one other lieutenant, three passed midshipman, and only one other midshipman—was pretty valuable. When Lieutenant W. F. Lynch was relieved in August 1845, it was "A. F. Warley" who was given responsibility for keeping the log, and it was he who had the deck on a rotating basis in port and at sea. On larger vessels only a lieutenant or occasionally a passed midshipman, would have been granted those duties.

Lynch's relief was Lieutenant Commanding William C. Whittle (later to command the Confederate naval station at New Orleans), and Whittle's first lieutenant was Melancton Smith. George Rodgers, acting master, and two other passed midshipmen were those senior to Warley. James I. Waddell (years later commander of the last Confederate raider, *Shenandoah*) was the other midshipman on this vessel, which proved to be a shallow-water challenge for the rest of the year.

The *Colonel Harney* was intended to be a coastal patrol steamer (with sail) to protect the live oaks and other ship-building timber on government land, such as that near Pensacola, and to carry supplies, primarily between East Coast ports and New Orleans.

In the spring of 1845, following the U.S. annexation resolution of Texas, the government in Washington feared for the safety of that potential state.

Mexico recalled its ambassador from Washington, and U.S. troops moved into Texas. From April to July, when Texas voted to be annexed into the United States, Commodore Robert Stockton was sent to supplement Commodore David Connor in the Gulf of Mexico, and six warships were moved into place, with four more en route. In late August the storeship *Lexington* carried four hundred army troops and artillery to Texas.

The *Colonel Harney* also left Norfolk at that time, but its cruise was more a detailed circumnavigation of the new state of Florida. Topping off its supplies on August 30, it laid in 5 barrels of pork, 7 of beef, 22 of bread, 1 of flour, and quantities of rice, sugar, cheese, molasses, and vinegar—along with 110 pickles. Inedible items included 146 pounds of soap, 30 cutlasses, 3 muskets, 30 pistols, 20 bags of musket balls, and 50 pairs of hand and foot irons.

The next day the ship was pulled out into Hampton Roads and tried the engine, which worked, to the relief of all and the quiet surprise of the engineer. Four days later, they stood out to sea and proceeded down the coast, stopping first in Ocracoke Inlet. Three days in Charleston Harbor was enough time for two men to be confined for breaking liberty and for five more to desert. Two deserters were recovered and received a dozen lashes each while Seaman William Seymour held up under six lashes for skulking.

On September 11, one day visiting and one grounding on the sandbar in the St. John's River off Jacksonville were ended by high tide. The next day in St. Augustine began a pleasant week, marred only by a grounding on the seventeenth.

The voyage continued to the small fort and settlement at the Miami River, where the ship took on a boatload of water and two canoes. The *Colonel Harney* proceeded through the Keys and around the Florida peninsula during the height of late summer to Tampa Bay; it went on to Apalachicola for refueling and passed by the naval station at Pensacola, arriving at Mobile on October 7. While the ship was in Mobile Bay, a large body of water with little depth, events provided all manner of training for a man who later commanded steam vessels of poor reliability in shallow waters. Along with some ingenious desertions by its crew, the *Colonel Harney* went aground, was inadvertently rammed by a steamer, broke free, and lost steam in time to collide with an anchored schooner, carrying away its jib boom and tearing off planks from the *Colonel Harney*'s wheelhouse. From this time onward, steam pressure and boiler leakage were continuing challenges. In the five days it took to get to New Orleans, both feed pumps and the manual pump were needed to maintain boiler water until a combination of river mud and bran, which had been put into the boilers, clogged the leaks sufficiently to maintain a reduced but usable steam pressure of ten pounds. This was enough to provide some level of propulsion without blowing all the steam through the seams.

In November the boilers reached a state at which civilian mechanics were brought on board to estimate the levels of repairs required. Repairs were finally begun in mid-December. The *Colonel Harney* celebrated Christmas by providing an extra tot of grog for the crew, an interesting gesture for a ship that had flown the ensign at half staff in honor of All Saints' Day on November 1.

War between Mexico and the United States was not immediate. There were preparations on both sides to be dealt with, and to Warley's surprise, they did not involve him. In December he received orders to become a member of the first class at the U.S. Naval School, a long overdue experiment forming at Fort Severn in Annapolis, Maryland. He left the ship on New Year's Day 1846, already late for class. Meanwhile the *Colonel Harney* was transferred back to the army in March, its boilers still highly suspect.

The concept of educating naval officers ashore had been proposed and been under fire for years. The obvious success of the U.S. Military Academy at West Point was evidence that a structured academic environment was excellent preparation for a professional officer of the armed forces. The argument that a sailor could not be educated about the sea except at sea was still the mantra for most of the old—and educated completely at sea— senior officers. Proposals for a naval academy had been scrapped in 1827 and again in 1833. Ideally tradition and progress should make excellent marching companions. More often, though, they have been ugly wrestling opponents.

Short-term naval schools were established in 1840 at Philadelphia and Norfolk and had proven their worth to some extent. Lieutenant Matthew Calbraith Perry had founded the Naval Lyceum in 1833 in New York.[8] Historians differ over whether this school was an early self-directed study facility or the precursor of the Naval Institute, founded in 1872 as an independent forum publishing books and a monthly journal, *Proceedings*. In the meantime professors had sometimes been shipped out on the larger vessels for the express purpose of imparting a useful level of knowledge to midshipmen. Service in the navy is a technical line of work. While experience was the only real classroom for the operation of a sailing vessel in myriad conditions, knowledge of languages was necessary, and navigation and gunnery took concentrated study. Moreover steam propulsion had arrived.

Finally, in the summer of 1845, Navy Secretary George Bancroft obtained navy control of a group of army buildings on the bank of the Severn River and shifted the Naval School in Philadelphia to that site. The school in Norfolk had been disestablished, and five school instructors were retained to join two naval officers as the faculty of the new academy. Some of the Norfolk instructors were fired, saving thirty thousand dollars, which greatly softened the budgetary blow when Congress returned to session. Congress reappropriated the thirty thousand dollars for improvements to the U.S. Naval School at Annapolis. The institution was now open for the first class to arrive in January 1846 for its six-month term.

Leading the United States in so many developments, the Royal Navy was slower to catch on to this concept of concentrated learning. Its first school ship was not instituted until 1857, and it did not move ashore for another forty-eight years.

A group of salty plebes arrived for the start of school on January 17, 1846. Most (fifty in a group of sixty-five) had entered duty in 1840, and there were five from the Naval School in Philadelphia who were a year or two senior. Ten youngsters in their midteens arrived directly from home. The "oldsters and youngsters" did not do well statistically; only six of their total ultimately graduated, and they were not considered part of the "class of 1840." Of the fifty members of the actual class of 1840, forty-seven survived to pass. As with any startup, conditions were harsh. Old Fort Severn dated to 1808 and had not been in the best of repair. Long Barracks, later known as "Apollo Row" and "Rowdy Hall" were used for quarters and for recitation. Smaller buildings, known as "Brandywine Cottage" (the old bakery now dominated by midshipmen from USS *Brandywine*) and "The Abbey," also served as quarters.[9] Remaining from army days and now used for training, were a few old twenty-four-pounders mounted en barbette (on top of the wall) and six thirty-two-pounders at the water's edge. Everything needed work.

On top of the usual problems was the enduring attitude within parts of the navy that this school was not necessary. This attitude was shared by some of the class of 1840, with their years at sea. (Later classes became known by the year they graduated.)

The class of 1840 fortunately did not gain the reputation later earned by the class of 1841, which was best known for duels and a small but loud near mutiny. While the plank owners may have been salty, they had not developed an "attitude" about the place. The course of study included those subjects that could be best taught ashore: mathematics and navigation, gunnery, steam engineering, natural philosophy, chemistry, English, French, infantry tactics, and gunnery.

In the course of everything else to learn was the tradition breaker issued by Secretary Bancroft on February 18, 1846, which changed "larboard" to "port." This order was navy wide and immediate. Though in use for centuries, "larboard" was sometimes misheard as "starboard," and the Royal Navy had changed to "port" in 1844.

Five days in late June were given over to examinations in all subjects morning and afternoon, with inquiries into general moral conduct and attention to study. Warley passed everything in the top half of his class and ranked twelfth of fifty examined. Richmond Aulick was first. Warley's poorest showing was in math and navigation, where he ranked twentieth. Not shabby for a product of the Pendleton Male Academy.

On July 2, Warley presented himself before the examining board. In answer to the preliminary question relating to indebtedness, he stated that he owed nothing. His age was twenty-three; his sea service was "five years aboard *Yorktown, Cyane, Raritan* and *Colonel Harney*." He apparently did not mention the months he spent aboard the *Shark* and the *Constitution*. The candidate produced journals of all his cruises and letters from his commanding officers. All was in order. He had passed the examinations. He was now a "passed midshipman"; accepted virtually as a junior officer and of actual use to the navy. A week later orders were cut for him to report for duty aboard the USS *Independence* in Boston. He was due there on August 1.

3

TO THE PACIFIC AND WAR

Aboard the USS *Independence*, 1846–1849

CONSTRUCTED IN 1814 as a seventy-four-gun ship of the line, the *Independence* did not work as planned. Maritime construction of that day did not involve extensive blueprints. Instead it often relied on half models of the hull, which were converted to drawings and laid out in an expanded size to form designs for the interior pieces and hull configuration. Many of the superstitions surrounding the launching of a vessel (coins under the masts, for example) were based on the need for all the luck possible to make sure the ship was still floating once it settled in the water at the end of the ways.

The *Independence* floated, but it floated low. Freeboard, the distance between the water line and the deck above it, was three feet and nine inches below the lower-deck gun ports, making them impossible to open on any lee application and risky to open at any time.[1] By 1817 enough experience had been logged with the ship for the recommendation to cut down a deck, or "razee" it, and thus reduce the weight. The disadvantage to this move was that it would remove a deck of armament in rating, if not in actuality, since the lower guns were generally not usable. The advantage was that it would allow the use of the lower-deck guns while lightening the ship, shifting the center of gravity downward and making a faster warship, as the sail plan would remain as before. This work was done, but eighteen years after the recommendation. The razee *Independence* was the only cut-down liner in the U.S. Navy. The British had solved several of their design problems in this fashion, and Americans learned from them once again, creating a fast, powerful fifty-six-gun frigate.

The razee *Independence*. From William Brady, *The Kedge-Anchor*, 1847.

On August 4, 1846, Captain Elie A. F. Lavallette placed the ship in commission. The next day, the Navy Department wrote Warley's warrant as passed midshipman. A star was added above his collar anchor. Minor uniform changes were nice, but more satisfying was his raise in annual pay, from $400 to $750. (At that time the secretary of the navy drew $6,000 per year.) On the twelfth the ship moved out of the Charlestown Navy Yard into Boston Harbor. Preparations were underway for deployment, and conflict was escalating with Mexico. Chances for action were best in the Gulf, in support of the army, but many independent opportunities for excitement existed on the West Coast. The Pacific was the destination for the *Independence*.

Still in steerage with the other midshipmen, Warley ranked number three of eight passed mids. The senior passed mid was the acting master, and eight lieutenants did the serious work. Only two young midshipmen were aboard to be trained and tolerated.

The ship left on August 30 with Commodore William B. Shubrick embarked. It bypassed Rio on the way to Valparaiso, where they reprovisioned and headed straight for Monterey, arriving on January 25, 1847. Shubrick relieved Commodore Robert F. Stockton as commander of the Pacific Squadron, shortly after Stockton had finished retaking California from Mexico, in concert with a small U.S. Army force under Brigadier General Stephen W. Kearny. A heated dispute over whether Stockton or Kearney was to establish the civil authority over California was defused by the presence of Shubrick, who generally sided with Kearney. Kearney then preferred charges against Stockton and against Lieutenant Colonel John C. Fremont, who had declared the independence of the California Republic six months earlier. Stockton and Fremont went east to deal with the legalities.[2] Shubrick stayed on as commodore and oversaw the renaming of the scruffy little bay-side settlement of Yerba Buena as "San Francisco," a much more fitting name for the wide-open boomtown it later became in the 1848 gold rush.

In early February 1847, as part of the plan to blockade and occupy the long, narrow finger of Baja California, Shubrick ordered the USS *Portsmouth* to occupy San José del Cabo on the peninsula's southernmost tip and nearby towns and to blockade Mazatlán, farther south on the mainland. The blockade was established on February 17, and by late March, San José and San Lucas were occupied, but not garrisoned.

Another leadership change had taken place. Commodore James Biddle, returning from the Far East aboard the *Columbus,* arrived with orders from Secretary Bancroft to assume command of the squadron. Bancroft had received information leading him to believe that Shubrick lacked the experience to handle the situation and that his command was on an interim basis.[3] Shubrick—embarrassed and possibly outraged—demanded to be sent home, since the secretary had so little apparent confidence in his abilities. Biddle, perhaps ready to go home himself, tactfully suggested that such a move could wreck Shubrick's career and that he should stay and serve on independent missions until communications with Washington sorted things out. Shubrick agreed and, after a trip up to San Francisco and back to Monterey, Shubrick, the *Independence,* and Passed Midshipman Warley all sailed for Mazatlán on April 20. Word had recently reached California, including the blockaders, about the capture of Vera Cruz on Mexico's east coast, by the joint navy and army operation on March 11. The lucky Gulf Squadron was winning all the glory while "we are just lying on our oars," complained Commander Samuel Francis du Pont, now commanding the *Cyane.* Du Pont was a rising star in the navy, a competent officer and also a political animal. A dozen years later, at a court-martial, he and Warley faced one another again under other circumstances.

On April 27, 1847, the *Independence* arrived at Mazatlán, joining the *Cyane* and relieving the USS *Portsmouth* of its blockade duties. The

Portsmouth returned to Monterey. Shortly thereafter, the *Independence* captured a Mexican schooner, the *Correo de Mazatlán.*

On May 10 Warley and six men were sent onboard the *Correo* at Mazat-lán. There was a fleeting hope that this ship would be an independent com-mand for the young man, but that was not so. After Warley had brought *Correo* alongside, seniority prevailed, and Monty Lewis became Lieutenant Commanding Lewis.[4] Over the next week, Lewis oversaw the provisioning and acquired a six-pounder cannon with all necessary workings, including twenty-six round shot. It was a good experience for the lieutenant, and Warley could only wish that it had been his. His closest brush with a com-mand at sea was cutter number one, in which he was sent off on May 12 after a small sailboat. He captured the suspect, returning the small boat full of fruit to *Independence,* where the cargo was undoubtedly sampled before release.

On June 3 the *Independence* once more headed north to Monterey. In July Shubrick again took command of the squadron and saluted Com-modore Biddle as the senior man departed for home.

During March and April, the First Regiment of New York Volunteers had arrived in San Francisco. In his last orders before departing overland for Washington, General Kearney had directed Companies A and B of the regiment to embark aboard storeship *Lexington,* hoist the flag in Baja, and take possession of it for the United States. One hundred fifteen New York-ers arrived at the picturesque white adobe town of La Paz on July 15 and reinstated the civil government on the condition that it remain loyal to the United States. La Paz complied, but to the north in Loreto and Mulege, local priests, primarily Padre Gabriel González and Padre Vicente Soto-mayor, were stirring up the locals to resist.[5] Mulege became a center of resistance in late September when Captain Don Manuel Pineda of the Mexican Army arrived with officers and soldiers and recruited ranchers to the Mexican cause.

On July 20, 1847, Commodore Shubrick transferred Captain Lavallette to command of the *Congress,* and the *Independence* came into the hands of Lieutenant Commanding Richard L. Page—a plum assignment for a sen-ior lieutenant.

Blockading of southern Mexican ports, once sporadic, now commenced in earnest with the frigate *Congress* and the sloops *Dale* and *Portsmouth* arriving in mid-September off Mazatlán, Guaymas, and San Blas.

The resistance at Mulege was tested by the *Dale* between September 20 and October 1, ending with a skirmish between Pineda's men and four boatloads of marines and sailors from the *Dale.* Mulege, however, remained in Mexican hands.

Shubrick maintained oversight of the entire California situation from Monterey and San Francisco until mid-October, when he sailed in company with the *Cyane,* back to San José del Cabo, where they joined the *Congress* and the *Portsmouth,* fresh from their relatively easy conquest of Guaymas. Their arrival at San José effectively squashed the most recent declaration of independence from U.S. occupation, which had been issued by locals on October 23.

Needing to secure San José but anticipating the storming of Mazatlán, Shubrick left only a small force to hold the town. Lieutenant Charles Heywood commanded a force of four passed midshipmen and twenty marines armed with a nine-pounder carronade and seventy-five carbines. One of the junior officers was Warley. This small command occupied a *cuartel,* or barracks, in an old mission on a rise of land at the north end of the town.

On November 10 the *Independence,* the *Congress* and the *Cyane,* all at action quarters, approached the port of Mazatlán. Meeting no resistance, a shore party of five hundred sailors and one hundred marines landed, seized and fortified the Mazatlán barracks, and then took over the town.

Five days later Captain Pineda, with an estimated 300 men, attacked 150 of the New York Volunteers at La Paz. Almost simultaneously 150 of Pineda's troops attacked the naval defenders of San José, who had fortunately been reinforced by 20 Baja California Volunteers. The use of light artillery saved the day in both cases, with the New Yorkers forcing off their adversaries. Heywood and his men held on until the appearance of two whaling vessels in the harbor convinced the Mexicans that warship reinforcements had arrived, and they retreated.[6] Mexican casualties were reported as six or twelve, depending on the source. The U.S. forces, however, lost none.

Heywood and his passed midshipmen, now supplemented by seven more marines, fifteen seamen volunteers from the *Portsmouth* and a few Baja California Volunteers, had acquired three fieldpieces and were stranded in San José for two months with only one month's rations. Their most recent backup, the *Portsmouth,* left for home on January 4, 1848. It was not long before Pineda gathered the nerve and the men, 330 loyalists and an unknown number of Yaqui Indians, to lay siege to the camp.

On January 22 they seized Warley, Passed Midshipman James M. Duncan, and a small working party who were hauling supplies from the beach to the *cuartel.* There were about seventy military personnel, plus fifty women and children in the *cuartel,* not nearly enough force to consider a rescue attempt. (The civilians had been taken in as refugees, being forced out of their homes for being possibly—in the eyes of the Mexicans—too friendly to the invaders.)

The American prisoners had the potential to be used as leverage for future negotiations, but they were presently only an inconvenience to their Mexican captors. Pineda had them sent under guard to Santiago, some thirty-five miles north. Warley reflected that at least he was not likely to die in combat and that the fates of those left behind were less certain. The badly outnumbered garrison was short of food and water and suffering from fever and dysentery.

Numbers prevailed for a time, and the Mexican forces took over the town of San José, except for the *cuartel.* On February 10 Passed Midshipman Tenant McLanahan, then second in command, was shot by a sniper. He died in two hours. The next day the loyalists captured the garrison's water supply. Hope for the defenders, already on short rations of food and water, was fading. In desperation they began to dig a new well.

Having heard of their difficulty, the USS *Cyane* arrived at sundown on the fourteenth. The next morning, 102 men landed two miles down the road and advanced to meet Heywood and 30 of his men, who had sallied out of the *cuartel.* The Mexicans retreated in the face of the advancing Americans, and the twenty day siege was lifted. During this time 3 of Heywood's men had been killed and 8 captured. The Mexicans lost from 13 to 35 men, depending on the source.

None of this had an immediate effect on Warley and his men, who were getting information on events. Warley was also doing some intelligence work of his own, gaining a perspective on the local outlook and developing a profile of locals' attitudes toward the Mexican Army. From the perspective of a twenty-five-year-old—one who had been around—he concluded that the local ranchers and peasants had had enough of Pineda and his band. In a letter that he managed to get out to Lieutenant Heywood in San José on March 6, 1848, Warley said that the people in Santiago, to a man, "hate Pineda most thoroughly." "For the sake of the suffering people, for the honor of the American arms, for revenge for McLanahan, I beg you to use your utmost endeavors to induce the Commodore to rid the country of a band of robbers." He felt that a raid into the country would raise at least three hundred locals to join them. Warley may also have earnestly felt that such a major expedition would also have rescued him and his fellow captives. He went on to say that Pineda was presently in San Antonio and

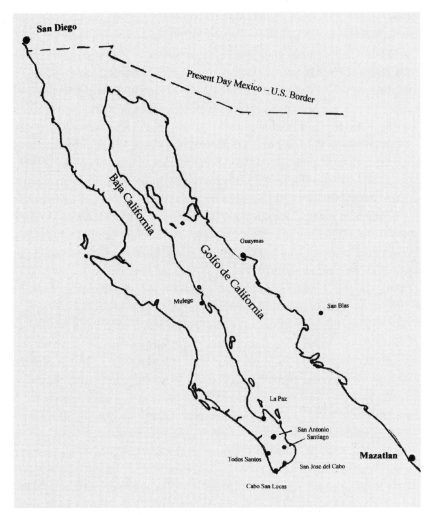

Baja California, 1847–48. Collection of the author.

that he was probably heading to Mulege "as soon as possible for he is not safe even with his own troops."[7]

As it developed, the navy did not launch a major invasion just yet. Pineda did not immediately leave for Mulege, and Warley was moved to San Antonio. Word of the prisoners' arrival in San Antonio, which was the local Mexican Army headquarters, had been received by the American detachment in the seaport town of La Paz. On March 15 a raiding party of thirty-four, led by Captain Seymour G. Steele of the New York Volunteers, left on a night march to San Antonio with the express purpose of attacking the headquarters and freeing the prisoners of war. Achieving total surprise, they charged the camp early in the morning, killed three, captured three, and drove off the others, including Captain Pineda in his nightclothes. The captives were rescued and returned to La Paz, where Warley, Duncan, two marines, and one sailor were put on a schooner for San José the next day.

At San José, Warley reported aboard the *Cyane,* where he borrowed uniform clothing, procured arms, and then assisted Heywood back in the *cuartel.* Among the "tidying up" duties of returning to his own people was a letter passed up through the ranks via Lieutenant Heywood.

While held captive, Warley had come to know Padre Gabriel González, one of those active in stirring up the ranchers against the U.S. invasion. Warley had enjoyed long talks with the priest. Now, with the tide turning against the Mexican government, which González had so ardently supported, the padre became fearful of his status as outlaw and expressed a desire to turn himself in. He was just as fearful, however, of Lieutenant Colonel Henry Stanton Burton of the New York Volunteers, who had all but put a price on his head. González appealed to Warley to intercede. This he did, writing to Commander du Pont on March 27: "Mr. Heywood enclosed you a letter from Padre Gabriel to me. I think it my duty as a return for the kindness rec'd from Padre G. to state that while a prisoner in San Antonio, Padre G. and myself had many conversations in all of which he expressed himself warmly in favor of peace and strongly opposed to Pineda but treated us [the prisoners] with the greatest consideration, even giving our men money to procure provisions when a report was rife that we were ill supplied. His letter appears to be sent for the purpose of finding out the disposition of the officers in command here relative to himself. I only ask that he may be informed that when he comes here he will receive kind treatment in return for his kindness to us and be left to the disposal of Col. Burton."[8]

Padre Gabriel's proactive move was prudent, as a week later two more companies of the First New York arrived on the storeship *Isabella* in La Paz. This gave Burton the flexibility to hold La Paz and to go hunting. He and 217 men moved down the peninsula, sweeping through San Antonio, where they captured Pineda. Then they proceeded to the west coast, to Todos Santos, where they subdued an enemy force of between two hundred and three hundred and returned to La Paz with 110 prisoners. By mid-April all insurgents had been captured or dispersed, and the area was pacified.

On the evening of April 28—almost six months after Warley went ashore in San José—the *Cyane* rejoined the *Independence* in Mazatlán. That night in the eight-to-midnight entry, the *Independence* log announced that Lieutenant Heywood, "late Governor of San Jose," reported aboard with Passed Midshipman Warley. It looked as though things had wound down and were about to be tidied up. Indeed they had.

The war had already been concluded almost three months earlier, at least on paper. The Treaty of Guadalupe Hidalgo had been signed in Mexico City on February 2. To compound the frustration of those who had spent the past eighteen months blockading and fighting in Baja California, it had generally been understood that Baja would transfer with Alta California to U.S. control. This concept had been expressed by the president and all naval squadron commodores. It was also desired by most of the major landowners and people of influence in Baja, as the stability of rule under U.S. law was preferable to them as compared to the whims of the Mexican military. But it was not to be. Diplomacy afar often differs from understandings in the field. Quite a few sympathizers to the American invaders were taken north as refugees at their own request and for their own safety, as the control of Baja California remained with the government of Mexico.

Results of the Mexican-American War included an increase in the area of United States by five hundred thousand square miles at a direct cost of $58 million, plus the $15 million paid to Mexico for lands ceded under the peace treaty. These figures did not include the estimated $64 million to be paid out in pensions or the human costs: 2,000 deaths in combat, 11,000 deaths from disease, and 9,000 desertions.[9]

Commodore Thomas ap Catesby Jones, who had made the precipitous capture of California four years too early, returned to the scene of his impetuous decision on May 6, aboard the ship *Ohio,* once more commodore of the Pacific Squadron.

While great distances had been sailed and a segment of a major war had been fought, the cruise of the *Independence* still had a year to complete. In the meantime there was the problem of rats. Attempts to keep new ones off the vessel helped, but the ones already there bred well and were unhealthy, destructive, and dangerous traveling companions. They could live almost anywhere and often hid in the ballast, which collected filth of its own accord. They gnawed through casks and crates to find food and could gnaw through bulkheads to get at the casks and crates. Ships' bread rooms, in fact, were tightly and completely tinned as protection against them.

When a captain had endured enough of the rats, often late in a cruise, he would try to find a fairly secluded place and move the crew ashore. Hatches, gun ports, air vents were closed and caulked. Charcoal fires were lit along the berth decks and in the hold on platforms of sand. The resulting carbonic-acid gas would form and sink through the lighter atmosphere, driving the rats up to where tubs of water were placed on the berth decks. After two days and nights, the crew could return to clear the stench, finding hundreds of rats drowned in the tubs and many expired in the storerooms. None was ever found in the hold.

In early May 1848, after almost six months in Mazatlán, Lieutenant Commanding Page shook the sails loose on his razee and sailed three days up to San Blas and then back to Mazatlán, La Paz, and Mazatlán again, as though he were testing the ship, its crew, and his own command afloat. In late June he put his stern cabin toward Mexico and arrived in Hilo, Hawaii, on August 12. There he allowed forty-four men liberty for a day and had them all return. Emboldened by his success, he sent seventy-six men and the bandsmen ashore for forty-eight hours and then allowed all Catholics to go ashore the following Sunday for mass. In the meantime a lot of vegetables were brought aboard. Warley, after spending his year and a half in upper and lower California, was again fascinated with the sights and smells of the tropical islands. He enjoyed the five weeks in Hawaii, even after the ship sailed to Honolulu. Honolulu had not yet blossomed. In the mid-1840s this town in a beautiful anchorage was still the hub of whalers and the trading craft that visited the California coast. It had a fort, "a few good houses, many huts and not a few tents,"[10] but there was increased civilization, and it was a bit calmer now than it was on Warley's previous visit in 1841. Yet it was still rowdy enough for several men to push the limits of liberty and desert.

After Hawaii, they weighed anchor on September 21 for Tahiti. Once in Tahiti's enticing harbor, they entertained the governor, saluting him with fifteen guns. The commodore went visiting among the French vessels, saluting them with thirteen guns apiece. The British consul came to call and was greeted with a nine-gun salute. When seaman William Gaddis deserted from the fourth cutter and was returned, he received twelve lashes.[11]

After ten days in Tahiti, facing the wrong wind at five in the morning on November 14, the *Independence* was pulled to sea by the ship's boats and those of the French squadron. It headed south and east.

Routine returned; the various divisions (two per day) were exercised at the "great guns"; Henry Thompson received twelve lashes for smuggling liquor. But ten days out, the nonroutine cry of "man overboard" broke the monotony. Immediately the full-time watch at the quarterdeck cut away life buoys to establish position, and the ship heaved to. Ordinary Seaman William Willson was thought to have fallen from aloft into the water, but as the ship came about, it was discovered that he had fallen into the main top. He was lowered and taken below, where he shortly died from injuries sustained in the fall. He was committed to the sea the next day. They never recovered the buoys.

The ship continued south in the topsy-turvy world of December summertime until it was far south of Valparaiso, the next port. Soon they joined the Peru Current and swooped up the South American coast. On December 20, just off Valparaiso, they "furled royals and flying jib" and spoke to the American steamer *California* from New York via Rio, receiving a mailbag for the U.S. Pacific Squadron, which they carried into port that afternoon. Many men received liberty in that Chilean port over the next four weeks. Undoubtedly this had a bearing on the New Year's Day observance, which, according to the ship's log, included the punishment of twelve men for either drunkenness or "leaving the boat."

When they pulled out of Valparaiso, Lieutenant Isaac N. Brown, who had the deck, asked, Warley if he noticed that the ship was headed north. Warley cannot have been pleased. Backtracking on what was supposedly a homeward voyage is painful for all hands, but time was not up yet, and the *Independence,* with its commodore, had station time to contribute. The next stop was Callao—actually San Lorenzo Island, near the Callao harbor entrance, where they spent several hours stuck on Whales Back Shoal, finally accepting help from boats of the British frigate *Constance.*

After two weeks in Callao and a total of 113 gun salutes, the *Independence* finally headed in the direction of home, stopping again in Valparaiso, where it assisted in repairing several vessels that had rounded Cape Horn. The *Independence* then rounded the horn itself, much faster than on its westward passage. On the first of May it was at the point where a port call at Rio was considered. Provisions were sufficient, and the winds allowed the fast sailing razee to buck the Brazil Current up the South American coast to the end of the voyage. It was time to head for home. They did not stop in Rio.

On May 21, 1849, the USS *Independence* "discovered Cape Henry Lighthouse on the port bow" and entered Hampton Roads two days later, taking up moorings at the naval hospital in Portsmouth. Orders dated May 23 detached Passed Midshipman Warley and granted him three months' leave. He went home to Pendleton.

He had summer at home with the family and was put to work overseeing the crops. Before the cotton could be picked, he had orders again, this time for shore. Warley and two other passed midshipmen, fairly bright students all, were to report to Commodore Lewis Warrington, chief of the Bureau of Ordnance and Gunnery, for duty at the Naval Observatory. They were going to work for the world famous Lieutenant Matthew Fontaine Maury.

4

SHORE DUTY AND BACK TO SEA

The Naval Observatory, the USS *Jamestown*,
and the USS *Savannah*, 1849–1856

THE NAVAL OBSERVATORY had its origins in the Depot of Charts and Instruments, founded in 1830 as the center for navigation and the shop for testing and maintenance of the U.S. Navy's fifty or so chronometers, the exactness of which was crucial to the determination of longitude. The establishment of latitude, assuming the opportunity for a star shot, was relatively easy. Longitude measurement relied on an exact rollback to Greenwich mean time and required long-term precise timekeeping, a capability finally achieved when Harrison's Chronometer was invented in England in 1757. It had taken many years before the United States Navy had accepted chronometers as reliable enough for formal acceptance, and they were not brought into official service until 1820.

The Depot of Charts and Instruments was founded in 1830. Lieutenant Louis M. Goldsborough was in charge first. Then the brilliant and volatile Lieutenant Charles Wilkes took it over in 1833 and ran it as his personal fiefdom until he left with the U.S. Exploring Expedition (known as the "Ex-Ex") in 1838.[1]

The depot became the U.S. Naval Observatory in 1842, with a new home completed in 1844 on a hill near Foggy Bottom; a new superintendent, Lieutenant Matthew Fontaine Maury; and a new direction. It was the first permanent astronomical observatory in the Western Hemisphere. Lieutenant Maury, as he became known internationally, gave direction and renown to the observatory with his development of usable wind and current calculations. In 1848 Maury published *The Abstract Log for the Use of*

Captain French Forrest
in his Confederate
naval uniform. From
J. Thomas Scharf, *History of the Confederate
States Navy,* 1887.

American Navigators, then the first of eight volumes of *Sailing Instructions.*
Focus shifted from the heavens to the seas. In fact no astronomical publications were produced at all from 1850 to 1861.[2] Mariners the world over
sent in their observations for inclusion in the *Sailing Instructions.* To adapt
the observations to data and to function, the superintendent required number crunchers. Thus junior officers of mathematical promise were rotated
through on shore duty. (The observatory moved to Massachusetts Avenue,
N.W., in 1893 and later become the home of the chief of naval operations
and still later the vice president.)

When Passed Midshipman Warley arrived there in September of 1849,
the staff of the Naval Observatory consisted of Maury and four other lieutenants, seven professors, and eleven passed midshipmen. Warley ranked
fifth among his peers. At this point in he career, his service record did not
list his qualifications gained or the time he spent as a prisoner of war. It cut
to the quick: total time in the service—nine years, ten months; sea—seven
years, nine months; shore—one year, three months; and unemployed—
eight months. While these months and years may not add up to his true
time in service, this service record was official.

Warley was twenty-eight years old and seasoned. His career was well underway—if somewhat spotty. For at least a year he would be in the nation's capital, and there he met Emily Forrest.

Captain French Forrest of the U.S. Navy, was a native Virginian with a good combat reputation from Mexico and was highly regarded by those who had served under him.[3] His home was Clermont, near Alexandria, where he lived with his wife, Emily, a young daughter, also named Emily, and a twelve-year-old son, Douglas. The captain was a sailor of the old school, having started out as a midshipman at age fifteen in the War of 1812. He was now fifty-five, well established, and prosperous. He was also fifteen years his wife's senior and saw no problem with ten year's difference in the age of young Emily and the professionally and socially acceptable South Carolinian.

Alex Warley and Emily Forrest met and married within a year. The Reverend D. S. Pyne pronounced them man and wife on June 13, 1850. All seemed well. Miss Forrest had a bold young husband, and Mr. Warley had an attractive young wife, as well as a senior navy sponsor with a well-appointed family seat. On January 8, 1851, however, Warley was ordered to report to the U.S. steamer *Water Witch*. Circumstances, possibly in the form of Captain Forrest, intervened, and subsequent orders in late February held the young officer in place until April. On the nineteenth of that month he was ordered to Norfolk, to the sloop of war *Jamestown*.

The *Jamestown* was a well-built cruising warship of 157'6" in length, just seven-years-old, and a product of the Norfolk Navy Yard.[4] In its short life to date, it had carried food for the relief of the Irish potato famine in 1847. Its long life extended into the 1930s, when it served as a marine hospital in New York Harbor. Rated at twenty guns, it originally mounted four eight-inch-shell guns and eighteen thirty-two pounders.

In 1851 the U.S. Navy officer corps was stable to the point of being static, and its opinions were established to the point of being hidebound. There were 68 captains, 97 commanders, 327 lieutenants, and 233 passed midshipmen (among whom Warley ranked eighty-fifth). For a year pressure had been building in Congress for a bill titled "An Act to Promote the Efficiency of the Navy." The problem was the lack of any mechanism to promote an "up-or-out" policy that would end the logjam of senior officers who were unfit for command, or even physically unfit for sea duty. The stalemate continued downward to allow the continuance of passed midshipmen into their thirties and lieutenants past the age of forty-five. For those of marginal competence and low competitive spirit, this status quo was acceptable. For the capable and ambitious, it was grating. Their writings, generally letters home and to brother officers, reflected their frustration. The problem had been recognized by the lawmakers, but relief was not yet in sight. (For an explanation of the naval ranking system before 1862, see appendix 1.)

The *Jamestown* had been placed in commission in mid-April and was standing off Gosport in Norfolk when Warley reported aboard on May 1. A month later the ship was at sea, and he was standing regular watches while getting used to the personality of Captain Samuel W. Downing. J. F. Miller was first lieutenant, senior to Lieutenants Charles F. McIntosh, Roger N. Stembeck, and Charles Deas. Charles M. Fauntleroy was acting master, and Warley was the only passed midshipman. There were six midshipmen to "bring along."

They were headed for the Brazil Squadron in company with the frigate *Congress* under Commodore Isaac McKeever, and enthusiasm was limited. Not as bad as the Africa Squadron was the general opinion about Brazil. Few ports and limited activities were not as bad as almost no ports, much higher disease rates, and chasing slave ships that were bound to outrun naval vessels. Regardless of the assignment, three years were invested.

A port call in Madeira helped to break the monotony after four weeks at sea, but the boredom had just begun. It took thirty-eight days to sail from Madeira to Rio. Then they went on to Montevideo, Buenos Aires, Rio, Montevideo, Buenos Aires, and Montevideo. By then it was March 1852.[5]

Each port had its own challenges. Buenos Aires shoaled so gradually that ships had to anchor miles out, and even then boats would ground in the surf. A portion of the local economy depended on providing big-wheeled carts to meet the boats in the water and transport all visitors to dry land.[6] The city was considered one of the finest on the continent, but it was beset with the problems of poor local water (rooftop cisterns provided the best drinking water) and the *pamparos,* winds whipping across the pampa from the Andes and bringing an immediate chill. The local food was an adventure, including porpoise steaks and livers, said to taste like a tough combination of beef and pork, and ostrich-egg omelets. Each "coarse fla-vored" ostrich egg was equivalent to about twelve chicken eggs.

Montevideo, Uruguay, was just a hundred and twenty-five miles down the broad Rio de la Plata from Buenos Aires. It had sought to avoid some of its natural shortcomings as a port by the construction of a well-made iron wharf, an investment of an Englishman who believed that it would increase trade in the city (his argument to the town fathers) and establish a good business for the wharf itself (his argument to his banker). Unfortunately its completion was soon followed by a sixteen-year revolution (ending in 1852), which curtailed trade and ultimately ruined the investor.

The *Jamestown* spent from December 1851 through February 1852 in Buenos Aires, with the crew generally enjoying the summer and looking after the ship. The *Jamestown* slipped downriver to Montevideo on March 4, stayed for three days, and then sailed out to sea, ranging up the coast to Salvador, then known as Bahia. It was about this time that things began to go wrong.

Captain Downing was not known as an easy man to serve under, and the strong-willed Warley was not one to suffer silently. It took just long enough for the *Jamestown* to reach the Brazil Station for the two of them to learn that they were not destined to get along. For slights and treatment received, Warley sent letters of complaint to Captain Isaac McKeever, commander in chief of the Brazil Squadron. Following proper procedure, these letters were sent through Captain Downing, who forwarded them with the comments he felt appropriate. Finding his reception aboard the flagship, indeed throughout the squadron, to be increasingly chilly, Warley requested copies of this correspondence, assuming it to be the reason for the downward slide of his stock. He was promised copies but did not receive them.[7]

Finally transferred to the storeship *Relief*, Warley assumed that he would depart on it and head for home early but with his reputation in question. On April 25, 1852, he wrote the commodore another letter, in which he called Captain Downing "an officer notoriously with nothing to lose in such a contest [who] has with a recklessness peculiar to his position, attacked my personal character, with the most serious aspersions which, if true, make it due to the Navy, that I should be dismissed from it." He then further complained of the lack of response to his request for copies of the letters from Downing to the commander in chief.

Response on this occasion was immediate. Warley's court-martial was convened the next day. The frigate *Congress* and the *Relief* were anchored off Montevideo on April 26, 1852, and the court convened aboard the *Congress*, with its commanding officer, Commander George F. Pearson, as president of the court. Passed Midshipman Warley was charged with insubordination, treating his superior officer with contempt, conduct unbecoming an officer, and disrespect to his superior officer. All charges were based on the letter Warley had sent to the commodore on the previous day.

Rather rapidly convicted of all but the second charge, Warley was sentenced to be suspended from duty for three calendar months and to be reprimanded by the commander in chief in the presence of the officers of the squadron. He returned home aboard the *Relief,* reaching his bride in Alexandria in late July.[8] The rest of the cruise did not go well for the *Jamestown.* Captain Downing was cashiered from the navy in September 1854, after a lengthy dispute with his former secretary, whom he did not choose to pay.

Clermont, a working plantation of three-hundred acres, was located just four miles outside Alexandria. French Forrest had purchased the farm in 1851, bringing back into the family property once owned by his grandfather. In the intervening years, it had been owned by Sydney Smith Lee— brother of General Robert E. Lee. Captain Smith Lee's son Fitzhugh, later one of the most competent Confederate cavalry leaders—was born there. The farm had multiple buildings for lodging and small commerce, including a blacksmith shop, brick kiln, and stables as well as sheds to house cattle, sheep and hogs.[9] It was here that Warley now returned.

He stayed on at Clermont through most of September until orders sent him away from the frail Emily to New York as acting master of the sloop *Marion.* Acting master was a step away from steerage and a good posting, especially good in light of the recent unpleasantness in South America. While being the son-in-law of a senior captain was not automatically a career booster, it was not a career buster either.

Warley went north with trepidation. Emily was not well, and her health continued to decline. On October 22, 1852, he received orders detaching him on leave. He left immediately for Clermont. A month and a half later, he was posted to the Naval Observatory. Emily died in March, and three days after her funeral, on the twenty-fifth, Warley was detached from the observatory and given leave for Pendleton. He stayed until midsummer.

Often the best cure for grief is travel, so Warley was in the right profession. On July 30, 1853, the navy ordered him to the frigate *Savannah,* which was set to join the Brazil Squadron. Warley was going back to Rio, Montevideo, and Buenos Aires.

With no heart for shopping, Warley had to replace his uniforms. The Navy Department had made the first major uniform changes since 1830 and the subsequent modifications of 1846.[10] He had no need to purchase epaulets, the large metal shoulder boards with a deep fringe of gold lace that distinguished lieutenants and officers senior to them. He did need new full-dress and undress coats and trousers. While a midshipman still wore

REPRESENTATION OF THE NEW REGULATION UNIFORM OF THE UNITED STATES NAVY.

PURSER.   MASTER.   MIDSHIPMAN.   CAPTAIN.   PASSED MIDSHIPMAN.   LIEUTENANT.
FULL UNIFORM OF THE UNITED STATES NAVY.

The new U.S. Navy uniforms of 1852. Warley was then a passed midshipman (second from right). From *Harper's Magazine,* circa 1852; collection of the author.

an anchor on his collar, a passed mid left behind his anchor with star and on all uniforms wore a single strip of gold lace on each shoulder, instead of epaulets or shoulder straps. He still wore buttons on his cuffs, a convention with Royal Navy origins designed to discourage young midshipmen from wiping their noses with their sleeves. U.S. Navy commissioned officers now wore gold stripes on their cuffs that varied in number according to their ranks in a system that remains similar to this day. Lieutenants then wore a single three-quarter-inch strip of gold lace on the cuff while commanders wore two and captains three. The modifications of 1846 had cured the lieutenants' "list to starboard" by allowing them to wear epaulets on both shoulders, instead of just the right. This was not universally popular among the frugal, as the old system would let a man in the long, long rank of lieutenant get a lot of mileage out of one pair of epaulets. When he wore one at a time, he could save the best-looking one for inspections.

The *Savannah,* a contemporary of the *Raritan* with a similar twenty-two-year building term, was again placed in commission on August 9, 1853, in Gosport at Norfolk and moved to anchorage off the Portsmouth naval hospital. The crew consisted of 106 seamen, 91 ordinary seamen, 72 landsmen, 32 boys, 9 musicians, and 49 marines. Captain Samuel Mercer was commanding officer, and Commodore William D. Salter was embarked.[11] Warley was acting master of the frigate. In early September, they shifted anchorage to Hampton Roads and on the fifteenth put to sea, making Rio in just under two months.

Unknown to those stateside, in July Matthew Calbraith Perry brought his squadron of the *Mississippi,* the *Susquehanna,* the *Plymouth,* and the *Saratoga* into Tokyo Bay and embarked on the tedious and well-staged negotiations that were to open up Japan to the world.

For the next three years, however, the *Savannah* was in Rio and Montevideo. Not even Buenos Aires to break the monotony. Ever since the military uprising of 1852, Argentina had been in continual unrest and that port city had refused to join the rest of the country's government. The United States had to find a new "best" port. Except for Rio, it never really did. The Brazil Squadron, including the sloop *Germantown* (under Commander William F. Lynch), the brig *Bainbridge* (under Lieutenant Charles G. Hunter), and the *Jamestown*—until it left—went north and south, spending weeks, even months, at a time in Rio and Montevideo.

Rio became a fairly agreeable second home to officers in the navies of Britain, France, Spain, Portugal, Holland, and Brazil as well as the United States. Ships of these navies were in and out continually.[12] While this was a nuisance to the officers of the deck, who had to deal with constant senior-officer visits, saluting, and displaying just the proper ensign for each ship, the place was beautiful. In addition to the landmark Sugarloaf, Signal Hill, the little island of Lucia, the fortified Ilha das Cobras, and the well-named Hood's Nose were all memorable. The city offered beaches, the Valley of the Oranges, and Gloria Hill, accented by the belfries of the Church of Nossa Senhora de Gloria near the iron-gray Benedictine convent. A carriage ride down the Passeio Público could lead to the massive Arcos De Carico aqueduct, the emperor's palace, and the empress's gardens. Warley had friends aboard ship and was able to form friendly acquaintances among officers from other nations among the international gathering of maritime professionals. It is not unlikely that the widower became acquainted with the ladies ashore, but few records of such conduct have been left for posterity.

In March, Warley was warranted master, and in October he was sent a letter with his commission as lieutenant, to date from September 14, 1855. He was one of many new lieutenants, for the U.S. Navy had finally undergone the great purge that had been in the works for a long time. Warley took his place as sixth lieutenant of a U.S. Navy frigate. Passed Midshipman

C. W. Flusser moved up to acting master. By the time they returned from the cruise, Flusser was also a lieutenant.

The great purge was known officially as "An Act to Promote the Efficiency of the Navy." It had been a project of several in Congress since 1850, and it had been the fervent wish of many in the navy for some time before that. In his annual report for 1853, Navy Secretary James C. Dobbin had urged action to streamline the commissioned component of the service.[13] He repeated the request to Congress in 1854. During that session a bill to reduce the logjam of less-than-effective officers in every rank, passed midshipman and above, was passed by the House in early February 1855 and by the Senate on the twenty-eighth of that month. A board of officers to review the qualifications of all naval officers was appointed by June.

Chairing this efficiency board was Captain William B. Shubrick. Other members included Captains Matthew C. Perry, Charles S. McCauley, Cornelius K. Stribling, and Abraham Bigelow; Commanders Samuel Francis du Pont, Garrett J. Pendergrast, Franklin Buchanan, Samuel Barron, and Andrew H. Foote; and Lieutenants John S. Missroon, Richard L. Page, Sylvanus W. Godon, William L. Maury, and James S. Biddle. One of the most influential of the board members was the relatively junior Commander du Pont. Never far from the ears of his Delaware senators, Du Pont was also a confidant of the secretary of the navy and had been a major voice favoring the elimination of the "dead wood."

Service on the committee was not agreeable duty, especially for Shubrick.[14] It is never pleasant to decide the fate of your peers. The careers and potential of 712 officers were reviewed. The findings dispatched to Secretary Dobbin recommended that 49 be dropped as incompetent or unworthy, that 71 be placed on the "reserved" (retired) list with leave of absence pay, and that 81 be placed on the "reserved" list with furlough pay (one half of leave of absence pay). On receipt of the findings, the secretary sent for Commander du Pont to assist him through the review. After deliberation, the list was forwarded to President Franklin Pierce at the end of July 1855.

While these changes were generally considered good and certainly benefited Warley in South America by slightly accelerating his promotion, others considered them a public insult, most prominently Warley's former boss, the renowned superintendent of the Naval Observatory, Lieutenant Matthew Fontaine Maury. Public outrage made Maury its focal point.

There is no question that, when 28 percent of the professional officer corps of a major service is put to pasture by an internal committee, political outrage will be the result. It is obvious too that the newspapers would go into a feeding frenzy.

The board erred in applying the strict rules of physical qualifications to Maury. He was not completely fit for sea duty because he had a lame leg (and a volatile tendency toward seasickness); yet he was uniquely qualified as the foremost navigational mind of the century. He was already in the reduced-pay scale of a shore-duty lieutenant. The board now placed him on the reserved list with leave-of-absence pay and denied him the opportunity for promotion. Maury wrote to the Navy Secretary and began a public fight. With his political allies, including Senator Sam Houston of Texas, he took his case to the country, with the assistance of the press and the support of influential friends of other reduced or discarded officers.

The debate continued through the end of the 1856 legislative session. In the next session Congress passed the much debated "Act to Amend an Act to Promote the Efficiency of the Navy." The major provisions of the new law allowed all officers affected to request a court of inquiry at which they could show cause why their status should be reversed and their original positions restored. In the end 108 of the dismissals were reviewed, and the navy reversed the majority of them, including that of Lieutenant Maury.

In total 48 officers were finally dismissed, including 19 lieutenants. When the dust settled, Warley was second of 150 lieutenants promoted in the three middays of September 1855, and he ranked number 171 of 326 lieutenants in the registry. His friend and fellow South Carolinian Thomas Huger, who was five years senior to him, ranked number 71 among lieutenants. It was still a long time in one rank. At this time a lieutenant was paid $1,500 per year while a lieutenant waiting orders received $1,200. Though the pay increase was good, promotion to a commissioned rank often meant that new uniforms were required. With their striping and other adornments, navy uniforms have always been more expensive than those for officers in other branches of the armed services. The naval epaulets ($45), cocked hat with box ($15), and striped undress coats ($35 each) accounted for about a third of the $300 or more that it would cost him to be refitted. Some of this expense was deferred until his return to American tailors with a specialty in uniform items.

The *Savannah* spent the rest of 1855 and the majority of 1856 in the same routine of Rio, sea, Montevideo, and sea. There were just so many artificial flowers made of feathers that the nuns in Rio could sell to a widowed officer. Shore leave was what a man could make of it, and the last third of a three-year cruise was boringly like the middle third only much worse.

Finally at the end of November 1856, the tanned crew faced into the cold wind of New York, more than three years and two months after departing, and they dropped anchor at the Brooklyn Navy Yard. Secretary Dobbin detached Lieutenant Warley and gave him three months' leave. He headed for Pendleton.

Virtually all passed midshipmen had been promoted in 1855, and the Navy Register shows none left in October of that year. There were thirty-one midshipmen: sixteen midshipmen—graduates of the Naval School (now the Naval Academy)—plus the midshipman students at Annapolis. By 1857 this number had evolved to twenty-four passed midshipmen and thirty midshipmen, plus the students. The upshot was a temporary surplus of lieutenants, and the result was almost six months at home for Warley.

5

BACK TO SEA AND STEAM

USS *Mississippi,* 1857–1859

To FURTHER INDICATE Warley's need for duty, rather than the navy's urgent need for him, Navy Secretary Isaac Toucey directed him to proceed to the receiving ship *North Carolina* in New York on May 14, 1857. There was little glory or pleasantness aboard a receiving ship, but there was a three-hundred-dollar-per-year improvement in pay.

Two months later a full-time position opened for Warley with the untimely illness of John P. Decatur, second lieutenant of the steam frigate *Mississippi* nearby at the Brooklyn Navy Yard. Decatur died on July 17. Warley attended Decatur's funeral at the Naval Hospital and reported aboard two days later. In a month they were at sea, headed for the East India Squadron via the Cape of Good Hope. In a relatively short space of time, the new third lieutenant eased into some sort of working relationship with Captain William Nicholson and "number one," Lieutenant R. N. Stembel, as well as with the other lieutenants: Thomas Pattison, J. B. Sproston, and Henry Erben, the last two being junior to Warley.[1]

In addition to his primary job, which was usually serving as deck officer, Warley inherited supervision of the gunnery department, actually overseen by the warranted gunner. Periodically the gunner and his quarter gunners entered the copper-lined magazine, carrying safety lanterns and wearing slippers rather than their shoes, to rotate all powder barrels top to bottom to preserve the mix.

Having served aboard the *Colonel Harney,* Warley had been exposed to steam before, and the *Mississippi* also had some age on it, dating from 1841. It was a side-wheel frigate, mounting a pair of ten-inch guns and four eight-inch guns to a side. At 229 feet overall, its two side-lever engines (seventy-five-inch bore and seven-foot stroke) produced 650 horsepower and drove it toward its design speed of eleven knots. The ship had been built in Philadelphia, was rigged as a bark, and had originally been designed to act as a test bed for long- and short-stroke engines. Both the *Mississippi* and its sister ship, the *Missouri,* were considered successful and good steamers.[2]

Captain Nicholson brought the *Mississippi* into Capetown just two months out, after a week stay in Funchal, Madeira Islands. Nine days was all they had in Capetown, and the ship took the great westerlies around the cape up to Mauritius for further replenishment before the four-week haul across the Indian Ocean to Jakarta (then called Batavia), which capped the north side of Java's western tip. Warley regularly had the deck on this passage, and regularly had a problem with Quartermaster John Danson, acting as helmsman.

The long passage across the Indian Ocean is a navigational challenge. The voyage was monotonous, with Warley standing one out of every four watches, at best one in five. A lieutenant had the deck every day, rotating though different times with no landfall to change the view—and it was hot.

The ship's log indicates the course of the vessel for each hour, a convenience in reconstructing a dead-reckoning plot when sun lines and star shots are not available or need backup. Repeatedly Danson let the ship fall off course. Warley had called him on this before. Acting Master George Bacon had also observed this problem, and Danson had been subjected to the second worst nonjudicial punishment available. His grog had been stopped. The captain, out of character, had become convinced that the officers were "down" on the man and that the ship, because of its length, was generally unwieldy and hard to hold under sail on a steady course.[3]

On November 21, 1857, just a week out of Mauritius, Warley's low boiling point was exceeded. While on watch he sent word by First Lieutenant Stembel to the captain that he would no longer be responsible for the deck if he continued to be paired with Quartermaster Danson. The captain's response directed Warley to put the man on report if he continued to misperform. Warley replied that he would not put him on report and would not be responsible for the conduct of the conn (the steering of the ship) with Danson at the wheel. Having reached a disciplinary impasse, Captain Nicholson preferred charges against Lieutenant Warley:

First: For sending an insubordinate and disrespectful message to his commanding officer.

Second: For disobedience of orders.

Third: For using provoking and threatening language, while officer of the deck, to Quarter Master Danson.

These charges were left suspended over the day-to-day life of the man-of-war until a gathering of the squadron could provide the personnel for a court-martial. That did not happen during the two weeks spent in Batavia.

The ship weighed anchor in Batavia on Christmas Eve and arrived on New Year's Eve in the great port of Singapore. Now they began to gather with other components of the squadron, which consisted of the nine-gun steam frigate *Powhatan,* the flagship, commanded by Captain George F. Pearson; the forty-gun steam frigate *Minnesota,* on its maiden voyage, commanded by Captain Samuel F. du Pont; the twenty-gun sloop *Germantown,* under Commander Richard L. Page; the twenty-two-gun sloop *Portsmouth,* under Commander Andrew H. Foote, and the twenty-gun sloop *Levant,* under Commander William Smith.[4]

The *Mississippi* left Singapore on January 2, 1858, hardly enough time to recover from New Year's celebrations nor enough for a court-martial, and anchored below Victoria Peak in Hong Kong harbor on the twelfth. There they joined not only the *Minnesota* and *Powhatan* but the "flower of the [Royal Navy's] Baltic, Black Sea and Arctic fleets" that were just returned, along with the French, from their trip up the adjacent river to take the city of Canton.[5]

The Americans also found time and personnel sufficient to bring to a conclusion the charges preferred against Warley. Chaired by Captain du Pont, Warley's court-martial convened aboard the *Mississippi* on January 18, 1858. The trial was a bit unusual because of the positions taken by two stubborn professional men. Over three days the prosecution and defense presented their cases, and Warley submitted a three-page plea in which he denied being disrespectful to his superiors but emphasized that he felt that he had run out of options. He had put Quartermaster Danson on report to the first lieutenant three previous times, but still had to contend with him at the wheel. Warley also pointed out that he had not actually disobeyed the order of the captain, only announced that he would not obey one. This was a fine point, too fine to help Warley.

As the testimony unfolded, it became clear that not only Warley but also Acting Master Bacon had experienced continual problems with Danson's performance, his inattention, and his excuses. The captain always seemed to reprimand him and then return him to duty. If the other officers were frustrated by this, however, they contained it better. The court found Warley not guilty of the three preferred charges, but "guilty of refusing to obey the orders of his commanding officer." Warley was to be reprimanded by the commander in chief and dismissed from the squadron. Flag Officer James Armstrong remanded the suspension and restored the lieutenant to duty with a mild reprimand and the admonishment to "be more careful, circumspect and respectful to his superiors while in the execution of the duties of their office; and to remember that the first duty of an officer is to obey his orders." This outcome was not a blow to Warley's career in the official sense. Indeed he had been court-martialed before, in each of his two previous grades. The lasting problem was the gulf he had opened between himself and the captain and first lieutenant. Upon questioning by the accused, the captain had admitted that he had no complaint at all with Lieutenant Warley's performance and was complimentary of his conduct aboard ship—"until he refused to obey my order. I then altered my opinion."[6] It remained altered.

With another court-martial out of the way, thirty-five-year-old Alexander Warley, now ten years removed from his previous war, sailed into yet another conflict. He was destined this time to be an observer—with less chance for glory, maiming, or capture.

Attempting the expansion of trading rights and privileges within the huge Chinese marketplace, the British and French were in the midst of the Second Opium War with China. After years of these Western powers illegally running opium into China and taking hard goods and specie in return, the First Opium War had ended with the Treaty of Nanking (1842), which had ceded Hong Kong to Britain and given that nation the rights to five ports of trade. In 1856, seeking more ports and trade concessions, the Western powers took advantage of the ongoing Taipang Rebellion, by both assisting and pressuring the Ching dynasty with the grand mixture of diplomacy and force.[7]

Piggybacking on this enterprise, the United States had sent Ambassador William Reed aboard USS *Minnesota* to revise the Treaty of Wanghia (1844), which had granted the United States special privileges in five trading ports. Concurrent with trading concessions, Ambassador Reed was to attempt the establishment of a resident minister in Beijing to deal directly with the Chinese imperial commissioners and to clarify the terms of extra-territoriality—provisions guaranteeing that a foreigner was subject only to the laws of his home nation and could not be detained or tried under Chinese law. Extraterritoriality was a powerful incentive to foreign trade and a tool for merchants and missionaries, who were thereby made immune to Chinese authority.

The Americans joined the Russians in the awkward and informative, yet inexpensive and productive, position of being observers and beneficiaries of British and French efforts. They would reap equal treaty concessions along with the combatants. Captain du Pont of the *Minnesota* found it "trying . . . to see . . . preparations for active conflict & lay listlessly on our oars to the evident disappointment of the French & English, and without any gain whatever in the good opinion of these [Chinese], who have much more respect for those who drub them, than for those who stand by & see it done."[8] The Americans had, however, had some involvement in the conflict. In support of British ships in 1856, the USS *Portsmouth* and the USS *Levant* contributed to shells fired at the Canton forts and sent troops ashore to take them. The most recent taking of the Canton forts in January 1858 was an apparent replay.

On January 29 Commodore Josiah Tattnall relieved Commodore Armstrong of command of the squadron in Hong Kong Harbor and soon chartered the 450-ton *Antelope* from Russell and Company for the use of Ambassador Reed. Use of this ship gave Reed greater flexibility because it had a much shallower draft than the three-hundred-foot *Minnesota,* though he spent most of his time aboard the more comfortable, larger vessel.

The *Mississippi* remained in the friendly, slightly anglicized confines of Hong Kong another two weeks, enjoying the exotic atmosphere of the land and the hospitality of the semiresident Royal Navy. By this time it had become apparent that the first phase of the British plan to pressure the Ching government by taking Canton was ineffective. The emperor regarded Canton, seventeen hundred miles south of his capital, with general indifference. The second phase was for the British to descend on Shanghai, roughly between the two sites, and confront the Chinese with a show of force. The Americans and Russians would follow along, at least making the force look bigger.

The *Mississippi* weighed anchor on February 13, 1858, and eight days later worked into the shoal-filled mouth of the Huangpu River, just twelve miles from Shanghai. After two weeks there, arranging for Reed's upcoming, hopefully productive, meeting, the Americans were recalled to Manila, where Commodore Tattnall maintained a residence, and thence to Hong Kong to regroup with the other powers.

The combined fleets met again at Wusong, off Shanghai, on April 3, 1858, and the four foreign ministers met with local officials for the better part of a week in Shanghai until a note from the Chinese governor-general bluntly stated that "no Imperial Commissioner ever conducts business at Shanghai." With the intermediate options eliminated, the fleet now headed north to display its power at the approach to Beijing.

With the *Minnesota* temporarily disabled by a rudder problem, Ambassador Reed came aboard the *Mississippi* for the six-day trip north. When the *Minnesota* arrived for the negotiations eight days later, the two U.S. vessels brought to seventeen the number of the foreign ships gathered there.

Negotiations were to be held in the village of Taku, just above the fortifications guarding the mouth of the Peiho (or Hai) River. American observers to the conference closely studied the Taku forts on the way up and down the river and were generally not impressed. Du Pont felt that he could "take all their forts with my crew alone."[9]

The Chinese conducted their part of the negotiations with the usual obfuscatory pleasantness that sent pragmatic Westerners into teeth-gnashing resignation. Although a part of the negotiations, U.S. Ambassador Reed was not in a position to shift from diplomacy to action. His British and French counterparts were, however, and on May 20, bombardment of the forts on both banks of the Peiho began in midafternoon. The British naval gunfire took an hour and a half to silence the forts, which were then taken by French marines on the right bank and British forces on the left.

When river obstructions were cleared, British gunboats moved up the Peiho to unfortified Tientsin (or Tienjin), where British admiral Sir Michael Seymour moored his vessel at the entrance to the Imperial Canal, symbolizing his ability to deny Beijing its access to the sea. The Treaties of Tientsin, signed in June 1858, were the favorable results of this activity. Eleven Chinese ports would now be opened to European and American trade and a United States minister would be allowed, with the establishment of other foreign ministers, in Beijing. Extraterritoriality was also granted, as were virtually all the foreign conditions. All told, the Americans non-involved presence brought them valuable return.[10]

Lieutenant Warley did not, of course, participate in the diplomatic negotiations. Indeed, as soon as the fray at the mouth of the Peiho was settled, Tattnall ordered the *Mississippi* back to Hong Kong to provision. En route, on May 30, Warley was scheduled to have the deck watch of the frigate from four to six "of the afternoon," but because of a "sick headache" he exchanged duty with another lieutenant and lay down until six, when he assumed the other's watch. This exchange did not seem a major problem at the time.

Reprovisioned and rested, the *Mississippi* and its crew left Hong Kong in mid-June for Japan. Just four years earlier, the *Mississippi*, in company with Commodore Matthew Calbraith Perry aboard the new steam frigate *Powhatan* on his second trip to Japan, had officially "opened" the closed Japanese society to foreign trade and dealings. Now Japanese cities were on the list of liberty ports, with Nagasaki first for *Mississippi*. On July 5 Tattnall arrived in Nagasaki aboard his flagship, *Powhatan*, and found the crew of the *Mississippi* to be sickly. Cholera was an ever-present danger to Westerners in the Far East, and warm weather was its ally. Warley and his shipmates were ordered north to Hakodate, the southernmost spur on the northern island of Hokkaido. From Nagasaki on the southwestern tip of the largest southernmost island to Hakodate is a nine hundred mile northerly transition, similar to a voyage from Charleston, South Carolina, to Boston. The *Mississippi* arrived in the northern port at the end of the first week of August. Warley took the opportunity to go ashore and browse the local markets.

That evening in the wardroom of *Mississippi*, the conversation turned to the sights to be seen ashore and to products available for purchase, including local foodstuffs. Passed Assistant Surgeon Dinwiddie Phillips had also been ashore and had spotted a dark-green water growth that Warley said was "kelp." "It was not," insisted Phillips, "you shall not put words in my mouth." "You shall not contradict me so positively," was the line officer's unnecessarily heated reply. Chairs were pushed back and the two officers rose. "Blows and black eyes were exchanged," said a witness, who engaged in the business of separating the combatants.[11]

Fighting among officers—and in the wardroom—would not do. Charges were preferred. To Warley's surprise, added to "fighting aboard ship" was a disobedience of orders charge from May 30 in Hong Kong, when he had exchanged watches because of his headache. Resolution of these charges by court-martial had to wait until the squadron assembled in Hong Kong in mid-November.

The crew's recuperation from sickness held the ship in Hakodate for two months before it headed south for two weeks in Nagasaki. A one-day stop off the island of Amoy on November 2 was the only other waypoint prior to the ship's arriving in Hong Kong three days later.

On November 18, 1858, before senior officers of the squadron, Lieutenant A. F. Warley, by now familiar with the procedures, stood to the court to answer to his charges. To the charge of fighting aboard ship, there was little defense: it was done; it was witnessed; and it was indefensible. The disobedience of orders charge, however, seemed unusual, perhaps trumped-up. Specifically it "involved the exchange of a watch or the relief of a watch for Warley because of a 'sick headache' on the part of the latter, against the written order forbidding the exchange of watches without the permission of the commanding officer."

The court-martial proceedings lasted a week, from ten in the morning until three in the afternoon each weekday. Warley was found guilty on both charges and sentenced to be dismissed from the squadron and suspended from duty for the space of one year on furlough pay, "the finding and sentence to be read on the quarter deck of all vessels in commission before the officers on board and at all naval stations." Passed Assistant Surgeon Phillips received a reprimand.

In the usual straightforward manner, the ship's log from eight in the morning to noon on November 25 read, "Clear and pleasant weather with strong Northeast breeze. At 10 the court martial convened—Lt A. F. Warley was this day ordered by Flag Officer Josiah Tattnall to report to Capt S. F. du Pont, Commanding the USS *Minnesota* for passage home in that ship. Crew employed painting boats and their appurtenances. At 11:55 the court martial adjourned. Barometer 30.10—Thermometer 67."

At nine the next morning, Warley left with his gear for the *Minnesota* and at ten the court-martial convened to read the sentence to the officers assembled on the quarterdeck. The crew was "variously employed."

Being shipped halfway around the world on a man-of-war without duties and on half pay is punishment—especially for a man of active personality and limited purse. The festivities surrounding the departure from Hong Kong Harbor on December 8—with a thirteen-gun salute from Commodore Tattnall and rooftops and shipyards full of waving well-wishers—brought no pleasure to Warley. Crossing Captain Nicholson over the problem of Quartermaster Danson had obviously been a bad move that tainted all later interactions between the two men. The charge of exchanging watches without permission and therefore violating standing orders had come out of nowhere for Warley. It was enough to rid Nicholson of the pesky lieutenant and to show to him again that a subordinate does not cross the captain.

Reaching home from Hong Kong was going to take some time. Under sail as much as possible to save coal, machinery, and the health of the firemen, the *Minnesota* worked its way from Singapore across the Indian Ocean via Penang and Columbo to Bombay, where Ambassador Reed, still aboard and still an administrative irritant to Captain du Pont,[12] disembarked. Reed left the ship to catch a steamer through the Mediterranean and on to home on a flood of ship's officers' relief and along with a letter (in the general post) from Alex Warley to his brother Felix, who was practicing law in Darlington, South Carolina, asking for legal help in Washington City to investigate his court-martial. This letter arrived home only some five weeks before Warley did.

The *Minnesota* spent a month in Bombay, where the officers were entertained in royal fashion. "The only drawback was an excess of hospitality."[13] Hospitality was convenient for one generally short of money and now short of pay. Reciprocity was difficult.

The *Minnesota* weighed anchor in Bombay on February 13, 1859, and six days later anchored in Muscat Harbor, Oman. As the first U.S. vessel to visit the "destitute, wretched place—a perfect mudhole" in eighteen years, it was warmly welcomed by the imam, whose father had welcomed the last Americans. The "perfect mudhole," of course, was later found to be full of oil.

The long journey home continued via Capetown, and the ship finally arrived in Boston on May 29, 1859. The trip had taken almost six months, a full deployment in the terms of the gas-turbine and nuclear navy of a century and a half later. Warley's voyage on the *Minnesota* was just returning home from deployment.

Warley returned to Pendleton, where he again requested a copy of the proceedings against him. His brother Felix had asked a cousin, W. P. Miles, to recommend a reputable attorney in Washington. But efforts for earlier reinstatement were to no avail. Lieutenant Warley sat out the remainder of his year before receiving orders on January 19, 1860. He was returning to the Naval Observatory in Washington.

6

MAJOR CHANGES

On the Verge of War, 1860

THE PROXIMITY to his former in-laws in Alexandria was helpful. Warley also resumed a friendship with his brother-in-law, young Douglas Forrest, now just twenty-two, a graduate of Yale and a law student in Charlottesville.[1]

Even more important to Warley's future was his association with the observatory superintendent, Captain Duncan N. Ingraham, who had been a naval officer since the age of ten in the War of 1812 and who had gained national hero status from an encounter seven years prior in Smyrna, Turkey. There Ingraham, a fifty-year-old commander with his sloop of war *St. Louis,* had faced down the Austrian consul and the Austrian ship *Hussar,* which held Martin Koszta, a Hungarian who had been seized by Greeks under Austrian pay and imprisoned aboard the *Hussar.* Koszta had spent two years in New York and had publicly declared his intent to become a U.S. citizen. Immigration policies were not as formalized in 1853. With diplomatic backing, Ingraham demanded the release of the Hungarian and actually beat to quarters (calling men to battle stations) and ran out his guns toward the larger ship. The Austrians blinked, and Koszta was released to neutral French authorities. The Hungarian eventually returned to America, and Congress awarded a medal to Ingraham.[2]

Promoted to captain in 1855, after a mere seventeen years in grade, the Charleston native Ingraham was given a plum shore job as chief of the Bureau of Ordnance and Hydrographer of the Navy. He superintended the observatory. The two South Carolinians admired one another as far as their respective ranks would allow, and a bond was established. The captain

Captain Duncan N. Ingraham
in his Confederate naval uniform.
From J. Thomas Scharf, *History
of the Confederate States Navy,*
1887.

became a mentor to Warley. The following August, when Ingraham was
sent to Norfolk to commission the new sloop of war *Richmond,* he chose
the feisty lieutenant Warley to go with him.

The 1860s seemed to begin brightly for Warley. Although he had received his commission as lieutenant, releasing him from the purgatory of
steerage, the 1850s had not generally been good years for Warley. Now he
was heading to the navy's playground, the Mediterranean, in a brand-new
ship with a skipper who had his respect and enough in common with him
for mutual understanding.

Dark clouds sat on the republic's horizon, though, and they were obvious to sailor and landsman alike. The first 1860 Democratic Party convention, held in April in Charleston, South Carolina, failed to nominate a
presidential candidate. Then the Republican convention, held in May in
Chicago, nominated Abraham Lincoln, who opposed the expansion of
slavery. That June the Democrats met again, this time in Baltimore. There
the Southern wing bolted to hold their own convention nearby. The Northern wing nominated Stephen Douglas while the Southern branch chose
John C. Breckinridge as their presidential candidate, guaranteeing a split
Democratic vote and all but handing the election to the Republicans. Warley's native state had always considered the Republican Party as anathema.

Shortly after that party's founding in 1854, South Carolinian States Rights Gist described it "as a fungus which will continue to grow and ultimately elect a President."[3] The Republicans were poised to do just that.

By late September, as the *Richmond*'s officers gathered in Norfolk, they all knew things were drawing to a head, and most had made their plans. With Lincoln's probable election fewer than two months away, reaction by the Southern states, especially South Carolina, was expected to change the nation and all its institutions.

Warley had made his own preparations. His cousin U.S. Representative William Porcher Miles of Charleston, had with him in Washington, War-ley's undated letter of resignation, with the understanding that Miles would submit it on South Carolina's secession.

In the meantime there was a new ship to commission, fit out, and take to sea. With one eye on politics and the other on the task at hand, the officers set the *Richmond* to rights before it headed across the ocean. The engineers had the worst of it. The two Archbold low-pressure steam engines, with the huge bore of fifty-eight inches and a three-foot stroke, never worked well or for long.[4] The crew began to notice this problem on the deployment, but the upcoming war's demand for propulsion in new ship-building prevented any immediate change out. After the war the *Richmond* received new Isherwood engines in 1866.

Launched in September, the *Richmond* was commissioned in October and headed east. Since 1848 the Mediterranean Squadron's base of operations had been Spezia in the Kingdom of Sardinia, which encompassed not only the island, but a greater portion of land in what is now northwestern Italy. Spezia is located on the mainland thirty-five miles south of Genoa. It was agreeable in harbor and facilities. The squadron usually wintered there.

Conditions in Sardinia were much the same as usual, when the *Richmond* arrived, but at home things were indeed changing. Back in Columbia, the South Carolina General Assembly met on November 6 to choose the state's presidential electors in the national election. Rather than adjourn after their choice was made, the assembly stayed in session, awaiting the results of the election. Within the day the inevitable was confirmed. Lincoln had been elected.[5]

Before the week's end, the legislature had called for elections to a state convention to convene on December 17, and the entire South Carolina congressional delegation had resigned (although their formal letters were not presented until December 24). Federal judge Andrew G. Magrath walked out of his Charleston courtroom, leaving his robes on the floor and declaring that "the Temple of Justice, raised under the Constitution of the United States, is now closed."[6] Crowds filled the streets, proclaiming the need for secession.

On the eve of the convention, Felix Warley, no longer a practicing attorney but a drilling captain of artillery militia in Darlington County, South Carolina, wrote to former congressman and cousin William P. Miles reminding him to submit Alex Warley's letter of resignation as soon as secession was decided. Felix also asked that his brother be considered for a place in the South Carolina Navy.[7] Less than twenty-four hours later, Alex hurriedly wrote to Miles stating that he had just requested passage home for the purpose of resigning his commission. He also wrote that he had no money but would return in the store ship or "work his passage home" if necessary. He apologized for acting without first receiving notice of secession, but "I couldn't stand it any longer." In the same letter, Warley spoke highly of his mentor: "If the state wants a man, don't forget to urge the claims of Ingraham, he is the ablest Captain I have ever been with. I am not given to man worship but I like to do a man justice and I don't hesitate to say that I think him in every way an able man—one to take charge of a Navy if necessary—."[8]

On December 17, 1860, South Carolina delegates met at the First Baptist Church in downtown Columbia for the avowed purpose of declaring the state's independence. It was obvious that, while public opinion in Columbia was prosecession, it did not have the fire of unanimity. Among others the influential planter Wade Hampton was moderate on the subject, and many other Columbians had the reluctance that comes from looking beyond the immediate noise.[9] Any moderate in Charleston could hardly be heard above the secessionists' din. That afternoon, while the convention was organizing, a case of smallpox was discovered "almost across the street from the church."[10] A shop clerk is said to have brought the disease into town, and three, perhaps six, townspeople had been afflicted.

Immediately the climate in Charleston became more conducive to the health of the delegates—and the guarantee of the outcome. Early the next morning, carriages and foot traffic clogged Columbia's railway station as men jostled their way aboard the waiting coaches. Finally the exodus commenced, and at least ten hours of the day were spent in the trip via Branchville to Charleston.

In Charleston the delegates took two full days to arrive at the predetermined result and to draft the Ordinance of Secession. The work was done on the twentieth and culminated in an eight-minute, unanimous vote for secession. South Carolina celebrated, but some expressed a logical foreboding of what this "most necessary" action would bring, and others celebrated not at all. Benjamin Perry, a former Greenville legislator, resigned himself to secession, saying that, since Carolinians were "now all going to the devil . . . I will go with them." Charlestonian James L. Petigru, a well-regarded but out-shouted unionist, remarked, "South Carolina is too small to be a Republic, and too large to be an insane asylum."[11]

As a Christmas Eve present, Flag Officer Charles H. Bell, commanding U.S. Naval Forces Mediterranean, granted permission to Lieutenant A. F. Warley of South Carolina to return to the United States for the purpose of resigning his commission. Bell's order provided Warley with transportation home, giving him that much more time on the government payroll.

Warley, Captain Ingraham, and other Southern officers from the squadron returned home in January. Ingraham went to Montgomery to help form the Confederate Navy Department. Warley went to Charleston to command a battery of Dahlgren guns on a stretch of sandy island.

7

ONSET OF HOSTILITIES

On a Beach near Charleston, January 1861

WARLEY RECEIVED his orders home on Christmas Eve 1860. Two days later and an ocean away, Major Robert Anderson of the U.S. Army ordered his men to transfer from the indefensible comfort of Fort Moultrie to the unfinished and uncomfortable, but secure, Fort Sumter at the center of Charleston Harbor.[1] Considered the "first act of the war" by some, including the *Charleston Courier,* the move was not authorized by President James Buchanan, but it was the only strategically sound action for the garrison to take. Buchanan disavowed any connection to the move, but did not order Anderson to return to Fort Moultrie. Anderson occupied Fort Sumter with his sixty troops, sending the one hundred workmen at the fort to the city and raising the flag over Sumter the next day. South Carolina troops immediately occupied Moultrie and the small Castle Pinckney on the shoal called Shutes Folly on the northern side of the harbor.

Charleston had been preparing for hostilities since before the secession convention. Local militias had erected batteries near Fort Moultrie on Sullivan's Island and just across the marsh in Mount Pleasant during the second week of December.[2] Volunteer units, including Felix Warley's, had been operational full-time across the state. On Morris Island, a bleak stretch of sand that stretched south from the mouth of Charleston Harbor, heavy-gun emplacements were erected. There was good reason for positioning guns there. Sitting on a shoal that had been laboriously built up over the years, Fort Sumter was in the middle of the water between Sullivan's Island (with Fort Moultrie) to the north and James and Morris Islands (with Fort Johnson and Battery Gregg) to the south. The only clear water, with five

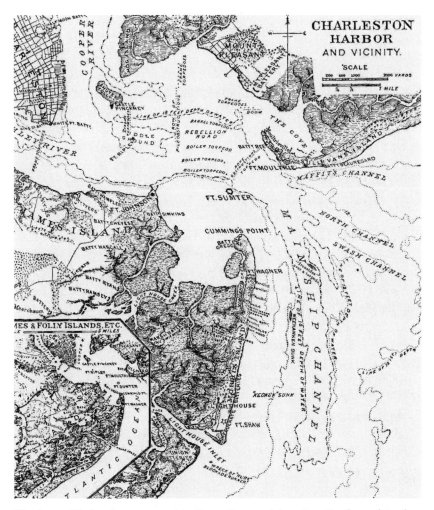

Charleston Harbor in summer 1863. From Century Magazine, *Battles and Leaders of the Civil War*, 1887–90.

fathoms or more, was between Fort Sumter and Sullivan's Island. Leading to this passage from the ocean were North Channel and Swash Channel. Main Ship Channel, the best marked and most reliable, came up from the south along Morris Island. Leading in from the north, along Sullivan's Island, was the year-old, recently dredged Maffitt's Channel, somewhat more challenging for navigators (especially when the markers were removed) and favored later by blockade-runners. With navigation lights removed, these shoal waters were tricky to cross by day and almost impossible by night. They were made even more difficult by shore-mounted guns.

At the northern end of Morris Island, Battery Gregg was adjacent to the Cummings Point wharf and a string of built-up embrasures, basically sand over an elaborate structure of boards and railroad iron. These fortifications were waiting on or were occupied by some pretty heavy guns—all trained at Fort Sumter. This had been the opportunity of those who had been, or aspired to be, military engineers; enough structural iron, a surplus of sand and a lot of available labor, some of which was owned and some of which was being trained, to move all that sand around. Three months had been available for the development of this enterprise, and as long as the guns could be found, homes were being constructed for them.

Brigadier General Pierre Gustave Toutant Beauregard, an experienced army engineer. anticipated a resupply of Fort Sumter in force, including a possible landing of as many as twenty-six hundred men on Morris Island via the Main Channel, which ran the 2⅔-mile length of the island.[3] To counter this force, which never came, three batteries were established along the southern mile, generally from the lighthouse south to Light House Inlet. These batteries, called Light House, Warley's, and Oyster Point, were two-gun units, Warley's being twenty-four-pounder Dahlgrens. The infantry dug their rifle pits along the ridges, and cavalry was detailed to act as lookouts and couriers and to swarm to those areas that required attention. The guns at Morris Island's north end, generally seaward of the landing at Cummings Point, were larger, more numerous, and destined to make history. They were aimed at Fort Sumter.

For the Federal troops watching from Fort Sumter, Confederate progress was obvious. Brevet Captain Truman Seymour applied his West Point training to document the defenses of Charleston Harbor from his central point of view.[4] His views of Fort Moultrie, Fort Johnson, and progressive scenes from February 13 to March 4 of fortifications on Morris Island indicate continuous construction of gun emplacements, eventually totaling eight, with places for at least thirteen guns and an estimated nine or more mortars. (The mortar positions were more difficult to determine from Seymour's vantage point because mortars do not require direct openings.)

Much of this preparation was in vain, for the Confederates lacked the actual guns to establish in the places created for them. The total hardware on Morris Island on the opening day of the war consisted of two mortar batteries, each holding three mortars; the Ironclad Battery with three eight-inch Columbiads, and a battery of two forty-two pounders and a twelve-pounder rifled Blakely, which had arrived from England on April 9, a gift from Charlestonian Charles K. Prioleau. They were a part of the twenty-seven guns and sixteen mortars that constituted South Carolina's side of the bombardment on April 12, 1861.[5]

Morris Island was commanded by Brigadier General James Simons, and his chief of artillery was Lieutenant Colonel Wilmot G. DeSaussure. Major P. F. Stevens, commander of the Citadel cadets—who in January had fired on *Star of the West,* a ship attempting to resupply Fort Sumter—also commanded the Cummings Point batteries.

Having worked his way south from Norfolk, Lieutenant Warley was accepted into the South Carolina Navy. His initial assignment was to command his own battery on the south end of Morris Island. It was situated channel side, where targets were less likely to appear than at the Fort Sumter side of the island, but if targets did appear channel side, they would be far more likely to be moving and more difficult to hit. His orders on March 6 were to take charge of his two Dahlgren guns and put them in best working order. The smooth exterior of the Dahlgren expanded back to a reinforced breech. Warley was no stranger to these guns, although twenty-four pounders were the smallest of the main armament that he was used to aboard ship. With a bore of 5.8 inches, the Dahlgren was not a bad piece of ordnance. Unfortunately its nominal range of just over a mile[6] assured that it had only small window of opportunity in which to hit a ship passing the gun's position.

Warley had five weeks to work things into place. Supplies were difficult to obtain. The sand was uncomfortable, but mosquitoes had thankfully not appeared yet. With a few exceptions, his men were unskilled; he began drilling them into shape. His old acquaintance and senior lieutenant Thomas Huger finally returned home to Charleston and assumed command of all three batteries on the south end of Morris Island on April 9, just as things were coming to a head. (In fact Huger did not receive his written orders until the twelfth, when the bombardment was under way.) By April 10, President Jefferson Davis and his cabinet had reached the conclusion that negotiations for the evacuation or surrender of Fort Sumter were not progressing and had small chance of doing so. He instructed Secretary of War Leroy Pope Walker to order Beauregard to make a last demand on Anderson for the evacuation of Fort Sumter, "and if this is refused, proceed, in such manner as you may determine, to reduce it." For the sake of finalizing arrangements, Beauregard delayed another day and then began the moves to initiate war.[7]

Robert Anderson was a Southerner by birth and marriage and had no desire to fight, but he was required by orders and honor to do so. He was also unable to delay for long. He was prevented from any sea-based resupply; small boats were patrolling the harbor all night to prevent local help; and his officers agreed that the garrison could hold out about six days, the last three without food. Beauregard realized the train of events that this small conflict would likely begin. Furthermore he had the utmost respect for Anderson, his old West Point artillery instructor, who had retained Beauregard as his temporary assistant because of his natural talents. Animosity was yet to overtake personal friendship and regard in the professional ranks.

At 3:45 on the afternoon of April 11, 1861, a rowboat carrying a flag of truce hailed the sentry at Fort Sumter. Colonel James Chesnut Jr. (formerly a U.S. senator), Lieutenant Colonel J. R. Chisholm, and Captain Stephen D. Lee—all aides to Beauregard—brought a dispatch from Beauregard to Anderson that read:

> The Government of the Confederate States has hitherto forborne from any hostile demonstration against Fort Sumter in the hope that the Government of the United States, with a view to the amicable adjustment of all questions between the two governments, and to avert the calamities of war, would voluntarily evacuate it. . . . I am ordered by the Government of the Confederate States to demand the evacuation of Fort Sumter. . . . All proper facilities will be afforded for the removal of yourself and your command, together with company arms and property, and all private property, to any post in the United States which you may select. The flag which you have upheld so long and with so much fortitude, under the most trying circumstances, may be saluted by you on taking it down.[8]

As surgeon S. W. Crawford, serving under Anderson, later so aptly put it, "Was ever such terms granted to a band of starving men?"[9]

In a manner no less generous to the character of all concerned, Anderson declined the terms and while escorting his "guests" to the landing, asked whether the harbor's batteries would fire without further notice. Chesnut replied, "I think not, no, I can say to you that we will not without further notice." To which Anderson responded, "I shall await the first shot, and if you do not batter us to pieces, we shall be starved out in a few days."[10] The gist of this unusual admission was transmitted from Charleston to Montgomery, where Secretary Walker telegraphed back that, if Major Anderson would state the time that he would evacuate, Confederate troops should not choose to use their guns against him.

Chesnut, Chisholm, and Lee returned to Fort Sumter just before one in the morning, bringing with them yet another Beauregard aide, Richard Prior of Virginia, who stayed in the boat out of consideration to the fact that Virginia had not yet joined the Confederacy. The message this time asked Anderson for the time that he would evacuate and thereby prevent bombardment. After consulting with his officers, Anderson agreed to evacuate on the fifteenth, provided that he did not receive controlling instructions from his government or additional supplies. Chesnut replied that there were too many "ifs" in the proposal and sat down to write out a message stating that the commander of the Provisional Forces of the Confederate States would open fire on Fort Sumter in one hour's time. It was then 3:20 A.M., and Chesnut felt the need to return to shore. They all parted amicably, Anderson shook their hands at the wharf, returned inside, had the troops roused, and the large garrison flag raised. Chesnut's boat rowed directly to Fort Johnson, where Captain George S. James, commanding artillery there, was ordered to open fire with a high trajectory shot from a ten-inch mortar at precisely 4:30 A.M.

An attempt to resupply the fort had been expected for days. The channel batteries on Morris Island were in readiness. Fire barges were anchored out, and huge Drummond lights were readied to illuminate anyone attempting to run the channel. (Drummond lights were illuminators burning a combination of hydrogen and oxygen to raise a cylinder of limestone to white heat. These lights were cumbersome and not easy to fuel.) Preparations were similar on Sullivan's Island. In the preceding few days, fresh, untrained infantry units had been shipped to Morris Island to counter the possibility of amphibious landings. Cavalry units were on both beaches as scouts and couriers.

In the time between the late afternoon negotiations and the telegraphic back-and-forth with Montgomery, a solid rain had begun about eight that night and lasted until around midnight. The artillery troops at Cummings Point had been kept at their posts, but finally sent to bed when the rain got heavy. A few of them remained in bed until the 4:30 mortar shot.

There was no doubt what the 4:30 mortar meant. The guns around the harbor picked up and began a hard concentration on the target in the center. Anderson did not return fire until sufficient light filtered into the casemates below. His heavy guns, thirty-two pounders and up, were en barbette—on top of the casemates and fully exposed. He would not endanger his gunners, even though these weapons were loaded and ready. The new Confederate gunners were surprisingly accurate, especially with mortars. All the return fire came from the casemates below, although some of the Federal gunners violated orders and snuck above to fire off the loaded guns once each—to some good effect.

The men in the channel batteries, some two miles removed from the action, knew what was going on. Even if they had not been informed by the signal mortar, the horsemen had brought the news. With one ear to the action and both eyes to the darkness offshore, they stood first on one pile of sand and then the other, hoping for the chance to contribute. Warley was impatient. He was wet and cold, and he was not in the action. He also was not alone in his impatience.

Offshore Gustavus V. Fox, nominally commanding the relief force for Fort Sumter but not the naval vessels involved, was aboard the chartered transport *Baltic* and was also a reluctant nonparticipant. U.S. Navy Secretary Gideon Welles had ordered Fox, a former naval officer but lately a mail-steamer captain on special government detail, to relieve the fort with the steam frigate *Powhatan*, the steam sloops *Pocahontas* and *Pawnee*, the side-wheel revenue cutter *Harriet Lane*, and three chartered tugs.[11] The tugs were to run in supplies while the warships fought their way into the harbor. All the U.S. Navy commanders had their orders directly from Welles. Not much happened as planned.

The *Powhatan*—larger and more powerful than the other ships but badly in need of a refit—had been detailed as flagship. Captain Samuel Mercer had the ship in the navy yard in New York when Secretary of State William Seward decided to make his move to save Florida's Fort Pickens and retake Pensacola Navy Yard. He managed to obtain President Lincoln's signature on orders moving the *Powhatan* from the Sumter mission to the relief of Fort Pickens, not actually in need of immediate relief. Seward found a willing ally in aggressive, ambitious navy lieutenant David Dixon Porter, who carried these orders to New York, unknown to the secretary of the navy or to Fox, who was depending on the *Powhatan*'s fire power at Charleston. The *Powhatan* was underway for Florida on April 6, out of reach for any help in Charleston.[12]

With two hundred troops and enough supplies to maintain the garrison for months, Fox had been some miles off the bar just two hours before the 4:30 mortar was fired. The only other vessel in sight was the *Harriet Lane*. The Revenue Service's only steamship, it was useful but too lightly armed to cover the advance of the *Baltic*. Of the three tugs chartered to do the inshore work, only one was available. Another had put into Wilmington, North Carolina, to avoid the heavy weather, and the third overshot Charleston entirely and wound up in Savannah.

Shortly before seven in the morning, Captain Stephen Rowan brought the steam sloop *Pawnee*, with twin screws and eight nine-inch guns, into the game. Rowan did not shrink from action, but he refused Fox's request to cover the resupply attempt because his orders required him to remain ten miles offshore and await the *Powhatan*. He was not "going in there to inaugurate civil war."[13] They could not hear the bombardment yet.

Fox, accompanied by the *Harriet Lane*, attempted to head in to transfer some supplies. As the *Baltic* and the *Harriet Lane* neared the shore, sounds of artillery and rising smoke gave notice that the war had begun. They came about and discovered that Rowan aboard the *Pawnee* had reached the same conclusion. The warships anchored at the bar in the Swash Channel and prepared to attempt some small boat runs into Fort Sumter. There were not enough boats or sailors for a significant effort. Fox was waiting for *Powhatan* to supply the bulk of those, but he would make an effort, though not that afternoon. Night—combined with the wind and weather at the bar and seaward of it, would make a precarious operation worse. They would wait until morning. In the meantime the *Harriet Lane* became the first warship to fire a shot in the great conflict.

Morning came with fog and heavy swells. The weather was still bad into early afternoon, when *Pocahontas* arrived, and its commander, John Gillis, took tactical command, being senior to Rowan. About this time Rowan shared with Fox a letter from Captain Mercer, late of the *Powhatan*, notifying Rowan that the *Powhatan* had been detached on "orders of superior authority . . . for another destination."[14] With Fox still stunned by this revelation, the senior officers agreed on a plan to send men and provisions to the relief of the fort after dark. They had hardly reached this decision when the *Pawnee*'s lookouts reported the loss of Fort Sumter's colors. The flagstaff halyards had actually been shot away, but everyone on both sides took this chance to find out if the battle was—or should be—over.

A boat went from Morris Island to Fort Sumter, and another went to Morris Island from the *Pawnee*. A steamer came out from Charleston to the *Pocahontas*. At 1:30 on the afternoon of April 13, after thirty-three hours of bombardment, a white bedsheet was displayed at the fort. Arrangements were being made to take the garrison aboard *Baltic*. The fort was a wreck but as yet there were no fatalities.

Fox placed the preponderance of blame for failing to supply the fort on the absence of the *Powhatan*.[15] In reality he had the firepower to make a run at the fort and a good chance at dealing with the shore batteries. Weather, timing, and the lack of tugs to do the inshore work contributed to the failure, but the *Powhatan*'s absence was a great convenience for the after-action report.

Anderson, the popular hero of the day, was brevetted brigadier general, later major general, and was sent to hold Kentucky for the Union. He retired before the end of the war, but he returned to Charleston exactly four years after surrendering Fort Sumter to raise on its ruins the same flag he had taken with him when it fell.

Lieutenants Huger and Warley were called to New Orleans, to the CSS *McRae*. With them went a commendation from Lieutenant Colonel Wilmot G. DeSaussure praising all the channel batteries and their attendant infantry for a "vigilance unsleeping and untiring." While Warley and Huger had not had the good fortune to be engaged in the conflict, they were at least mentioned in dispatches.[16]

8

THE RIVER WAR

New Orleans, 1861

As a warship, the Confederate States side-wheel schooner *McRae* was questionable. In fact it had recently been declared a pirate and seized by the U.S. Navy. It originally had been tied somehow to the Mexican Navy as the *Marquis de la Habana*. Compared to the emerging fleets of North and South, which included armored tugs and converted double-ender ferryboats as warships, the three-masted steamer *McRae* was relatively legitimate.

Its new commander, Thomas Huger, arrived aboard with his first lieutenant, Alex Warley, in late April. The wardroom would also include Passed Midshipman Charles W. "Savez" Read and eventually Acting Midshipman James Morris Morgan, who wrote down much of his own maritime history.

Read was a graduate of the Naval Academy and not considered a remarkable student. He turned out to be more a student of action. He found himself and placed himself in the forefront of some of the hottest action of the naval war.

Morgan was not yet aboard. Having left Annapolis just past the midpoint of his first year, he had traveled home to Louisiana with little but the Federal blue Naval Academy uniform on his back. He covered his uniform buttons once he reached the Southern states and endured the questioning, somewhat hostile stares of fellow train passengers.[1] After reaching his home near Baton Rouge, he applied without success to the Confederate navy and army, but he was rejected because he was only fifteen years and 5'5" in height. By July 1861 his persistence and family connections, however, finally

The CSS *McRae* coaling in Baton Rouge. From James Morris Morgan, *Recollections of a Rebel Reefer*, 1917.

had him warranted and posted to the *McRae*. There his boyish exuberance brought him before the gaze of the first lieutenant, well used to dealing with midshipmen. Following one of Morgan's frequent infractions, Warley sent the young midshipman once again to the foretop to spend some uncomfortable hours contemplating how he should have performed. Presenting himself to Mr. John R. Eggleston, the second lieutenant, with the first lieutenant's compliments and instructions, Morgan received the direction, "Well, sir, you surely ought to know the way up there by this time!"[2]

The captain and first lieutenant were both widowers, Huger's late wife having been a sister of Union general George Meade. Young Morgan was often the courier of notes between the captain and his new fiancée, who was living just off Jackson Square in New Orleans. Warley was seeing Miss Isabella Middleton Huger, also of New Orleans and distant kin to his commanding officer.

After a month aboard the *McRae*, having established the administrative details of his duties and with refitting still in progress, Warley realized that he would not see action soon. The *McRae*'s draft and mechanical limitations had already disqualified it from a role of blockade-running. It looked as if it was destined to stay on the Mississippi River.

Bothered by Federal launches raiding in the Mississippi Sound, the Confederate army called on the Confederate navy for assistance. Army captain Edward Higgins—formerly an officer in the U.S. Navy and now an aide to the district commander, General David E. Twiggs—convinced the general to send an expedition to clean up the coast. The Union launches were coming from the USS *Massachusetts,* which operated occasionally from Ship Island. When the *McRae* was approached for volunteers, Warley and Read were first in line. With them were Midshipmen John Comstock, W. R. Dalton, Sardine Graham Stone, and F. M. Roby, as well as surgeon Arthur M. Linah and several enlisted members of the crew.[3] Captain R. T. Thom with a detachment of fifty-five Confederate marines plus

The Louisiana delta. Ship Island lies just offshore from Mississippi City at the top right of the map. From U.S. War Department, *Atlas to Accompany the Official Records of the Union and Confederate Armies,* 1891–95.

one sergeant and thirty privates of the Louisiana Infantry constituted the landing force.

In the first week of July, lake steamers *Swain* and *Oregon* were commandeered. Warley took the *Swain,* which was fitted with a thirty-two pounder and a twelve-pound howitzer. Civilian captain A. L. Myers took the *Oregon,* with an eight-inch gun and howitzer. They sallied from New Orleans to Bay St. Louis, where sand bags were applied to their boilers for protection. From Bay St. Louis at nine in the morning on July 6, the *Swain* took the mainland, or inside passage, and *Oregon* the outside passage, probing for enemy launches toward Ship Island Pass. The coast was clear of the enemy, and Captain Higgins, acting for Commander Headquarters District Number One, indicated that Ship Island was well worth occupation.

The small flotilla approached Ship Island, a sand strip six to eight miles in length (depending on recent storm activity), eleven miles south of the coast at Biloxi. For years a major navigation mark between Mobile and New Orleans, the island and its tall illuminated lighthouse were now essentially empty. Ship Island's east end was semihabitable, covered in live oaks and cedar groves. Once, before a severe storm overtested their mettle, cattle ranchers had made a meager living there. The U.S. government never lost sight of Ship Island's value to the overall coastal defense, however, and in January 1861 the Army Corps of Engineers had been working to erect a masonry fort, another block in the wall of coastal defense forts that had been under construction for twenty years or more.[4]

On the afternoon of July 6, Warley's crew brought the boats' guns ashore and after much exertion, hauled them to the highest point on the island, mounted them, and built sand parapets for their defense. The masonry fort had not been developed sufficiently for use. Warley put Read in charge of the eight-inch gun and Comstock on the other. Midshipmen Stone and Dalton had the howitzers. Midshipman Roby (as Warley had no other gun to give him) acted as commissary and messenger. As soon as the guns were ashore, the *Oregon* departed for New Orleans to send dispatches to General Twiggs recommending reinforcements, ordnance, and supplies to hold the island.

From dawn to dark of the next two days, the Confederate occupiers worked to develop the fort. At midday on the eighth, a seventy-five-man company of infantry under a Captain Roland arrived to augment the original complement of ninety men and assisted in the construction of sandbag emplacements. Shortly after the sun went down, the USS *Massachusetts,* which had been on patrol in the Gulf of Mexico, approached from the seaward (southern) side. Commander Melancton Smith anchored his five-gun screw steamer some three miles offshore to determine why the light was extinguished.

Of an old army family with Continental Congress forebears, Smith was considered colorful by most current standards. Although slow to act without orders, he was a fighter and not cautious to delegate responsibility to his twenty-five-year-old first lieutenant, George Dewey, who went on to a long and distinguished career. Smith's careful spyglass reconnaissance of Ship Island revealed "three Secession flags, thirty-nine tents and four batteries in process of erection out of cotton bales and sandbags." He fired a gun toward the island, an act the Confederates interpreted as being a wake-up call to the lighthouse keeper for illumination.[5] It was not immediately acknowledged.

At dawn on the ninth, Warley directed Read to fire his eight-inch gun at the gunboat and Comstock to follow with the thirty-two pounder. At the first shot, the lookout on the lighthouse reported seeing though the mist a white flag flying from the *Massachusetts*. Others, seeing smoke from the funnel, correctly doubted the lookout's report, and their skepticism was confirmed by a thirty-two-pound shell exploding among them and throwing sand in their faces. A spirited exchange continued with no casualties except an injured leg on the Confederate side, but the Southern supply of shells was running short. Of the seventeen Federal shots and shells that were fired, several shots were excavated from the sand and returned by gun toward the *Massachusetts*.

Because the fog obscured his view as well, Captain Smith overestimated the size of the Confederate force as three hundred to four hundred men, and some of his officers figured as high as eight hundred. His count of the guns was accurate, however, and there is no reason to question his report that twenty-six shots and shells were fired at him from the island. Though Warley's report listed twenty-one, he may not have taken into account the shots his men dug up and returned.[6] A dispatch written that afternoon reported that Smith's men expended seventeen shots. Warley's account reported "thirty or more" shots and shells incoming from the *Massachusetts*, and it must have seemed that way.

In the course of the exchange, Captain Myers returned on the *Oregon*, bringing in the steamer *Grey Cloud* with guns, gun carriages, ammunition, and supplies. Taking ordnance and immediate supplies from *Grey Cloud*, Myers transported the equipment into the landing under fire—to the relief of the gunners, who had grown tired of digging for ammunition. The

Oregon and *Grey Cloud* then stood off, keeping the land between the gunboat and themselves. The sailors and marines quickly moved the ammunition and new fieldpieces up to the fortifications.

The entire engagement lasted about an hour. Then the *Massachusetts* withdrew after gaining little and seeing nothing left to gain. As soon as it was over the horizon, the steamer *Swain* left for Mississippi City to pick up three companies of the Fourth Louisiana under Lieutenant Colonel H. W. Allen, who arrived that evening to further fortify and take over the island. The navy and marine corps team, having done its job of amphibious warfare—on a limited scale—embarked that evening on the *Swain* for New Orleans.

A U.S. Navy study—developed by a group chaired by Captain du Pont and called variously the "Blockade Board," the "Strategy Board," or the officially innocuous "Commission of Conference"—had been under development through the spring and early summer of 1861. This group considered military problems all along the Atlantic and Gulf coasts. In the Gulf of Mexico they identified Ship Island, with its lighthouse and available water, as at least a partial answer to the need for a base of supply not too far from Key West and within striking distance of Pensacola, Mobile, Biloxi, and New Orleans. The first report of the conference, issued August 9, had as its first recommendation the establishment of Ship Island as the lynchpin of operations in the Gulf. Since Higgins and Warley got there first, Federal forces now had to take it from the Confederates.

Occupying an island a dozen miles offshore, dependent on waterborne supply in an environment of increasing enemy naval superiority, was a losing proposition for the Confederates. In spite of the July demonstration that a force of artillery and infantry could hold the island against an attack, the Southerners realized that next time the attackers could appear in greater force than a 220-foot, exposed engine, five-gun steamer just six weeks commissioned into the Union navy. And the Confederate navy lacked the number of vessels in the Gulf to counter even *Massachusetts*-sized blockaders in a resupply effort.

To show continued Federal interest, later in July, Melancton Smith once more took his command toward Ship Island. The Confederate steamers *Oregon* and *Arrow* headed out toward him, intending to draw him either into range of the shore batteries or (even better) to shallow water. The *Massachusetts* danced offshore, attempting to lure the steamers within range of its eight-inch guns. Neither side's tactic worked, and the steamers returned to the island.

The eventual outcome, however, was obvious. It was time for the Confederates to leave Ship Island. In September ordnance and supplies were loaded, and efforts were underway to destroy everything of value on Ship Island when the *Massachusetts,* in company with the sloops *Preble* and *Marion,* appeared and bore down, forcing an early departure before the planned destruction of thirteen shanties and buildings. Also left behind were a quantity of building materials and thirty-six head of cattle, possibly remaining from prewar days. After wasting a little time shelling what was assumed to be a masked battery on the now-deserted island, the Union forces took Ship Island for once and for all. Posted prominently on the fort bulletin board was a tongue-in-cheek letter for Commander Smith—dated September 17, 1861, and signed by Lieutenant Colonel H. W. Allen—in which the colonel remarked: "For three long months your good ship has been our constant companion. We have not exactly 'lived and loved together,' but we have been intimately acquainted, having exchanged cards on the 9th day of July last."[7] The Union navy based its Gulf operations on Ship Island for the remainder of the war.

While the Confederate occupation of Ship Island lasted for the rest of the summer, the volunteers from *McRae* were back at work aboard ship on July 10. Warley's concern as first lieutenant was the outfitting of the *McRae.* Almost immediately, the command went upstream to Baton Rouge to take on ammunition from the arsenal there. The *McRae* impressed the citizenry of Baton Rouge, unused to naval or even oceangoing vessels. It certainly impressed James Morgan, who joined the ship's company at this time. Still wearing his blue Annapolis uniform, he skinned the coverings from his uniform buttons. His blue uniform was not out of place. The other officers were still in blue and comfortable with it. According to Morgan, they "kicked like steers when they were afterward compelled to don the gray, contemptuously demanding to know, 'Who had ever seen a gray sailor, no matter what nationality he served?'"[8]

After two weeks in Baton Rouge, the *McRae* sailed back to New Orleans to take on coal. Uncertain of the future and his survival in it, Warley allotted ninety-five dollars per month toward supporting his family to the trusted hands of his attorney brother Felix.

The *McRae* then headed downstream. Its original mission was to be a commerce raider, but then the Union had set up its blockade of New Orleans.

At Head of the Passes, located where the Mississippi River reaches the Gulf of Mexico, navigators had an initial choice of three channels: Pass a l'Outre to the east, South Pass, and Southwest Pass. The first and third offered the best chance for deep-draft movement over the bars, and they were also far enough apart that they could not be covered by the same blockaders. By the end of the summer the Union navy had sufficient resources to block all three passes, and with some effort Federal forces had pushed inside and were patrolling Head of the Passes. The 233-foot steam sloop USS *Brooklyn* had appeared in late May at Pass a l'Outre and was joined a few days by Porter's USS *Powhatan* at Southwest Pass. Soon thereafter the blockade was augmented by the arrival of the *Niagara* and the *Minnesota.*

Raphael Semmes had taken the *Sumter* over the bar on June 30, after several days of waiting just upriver and sending the steamer *Ivy* down Southwest Pass each day to check on the presence of the *Powhatan,* which was no longer alone. It had been joined by the *Brooklyn,* the *Niagara,* and the *Minnesota.* All four blockading ships were far more powerful than the *Sumter,* and some were faster. Yet Semmes broke out and got away after a long pursuit by Charles H. Poor on the *Brooklyn.* In this instance Semmes outsailed Poor, even though he hauled about and gave immediate pursuit.[9]

The vise had tightened, however, and the addition of ships to the blockade at Head of the Passes made escape for the slow *McRae* impossible. After plying between Head of the Passes and the upriver forts for weeks, the *McRae* returned to New Orleans to face its future as the "station ship" for the city and the River Defense Fleet. Young Morgan was convinced that "northern leanings" of the pilots at the various passes contributed to their reluctance to attempt any bold moves during dark nights.

The Confederates still had the powerful Forts Jackson and St. Philip, some twenty miles upstream from Head of the Passes. Eighty miles beyond the forts was the city of New Orleans with assorted weak defenses. Light-draft vessels succeeded at minor blockade-running by sailing along the coast and through the bayous. While helpful for trade, these shallow passages did not replace the main arteries that used to accommodate major vessels. Much of the upriver cotton had been returned to plantations or placed in warehouses. It was going nowhere. Goods were not coming from abroad, and imports were becoming expensive. Coffee was $1.25 a pound; red meat was becoming scarce; and decreased grain supplies sent up the price of flour. Putting a positive light on the situation, the *New Orleans Picayune* commented in mid-August, "The health of the city was never in better condition at this season of the year," and asked, "Is the blockade of our ports the cause of the absence of yellow fever?"[10]

The Confederate States Navy had inherited far more than its share of "Old Navy" officers. Some outstanding, effective leaders had come south, but so had senior officers past their prime, men who had years of experience but lacked the ability to improvise when faced with new circumstance. Captain Lawrence Rousseau, commanding the navy in New Orleans, was faced with the enormous and complicated mission of building a navy. The area had many boatyards, but none had ever built a warship. Following the directive of the new secretary of the navy, Rousseau needed to construct ironclads. No one had ever done this before. He needed to take many vessels from trade and arm them as quickly as possible. He was in competition with commercial ventures. In the early months of the war, before the blockade, enterprising civilians had tasked the boatyards to convert various ships to privateers, and these individuals paid better than the Confederate government. Rousseau was also in competition with the Confederate army, which shared responsibility with the navy for the defense of New Orleans, and with General Twiggs's own opinions about the priorities for execution. Rousseau retired.

Into his position stepped Captain George Hollins, age sixty-two. Possessed with a surplus of energy and a fighting spirit, Hollins was in Naples, Italy, when Fort Sumter fell, and he returned home in time to receive his Confederate navy commission on June 20. Nine days later, he organized a raid on the lower Potomac and captured the Union side-wheeler *St. Nicholas*. On his way back, he captured three more prizes with the *St. Nicholas*.[11] His success was an attention getter for higher authorities. By July 31 Hollins was in New Orleans relieving Rousseau.

When Hollins arrived, he found that Rousseau had been busy and productive. He had procured the seven-gun *McRae* (830 tons), the two-gun side-wheel steamer *Ivy* (454 tons), the two-gun side-wheel tug *Tuscarora*, the five-gun side-wheel steamer *Calhoun* (500 tons), the side-wheel tug *Jackson* (formerly the *Yankee*) with two pivot thirty-two pounders, and the converted revenue cutter *Pickens* with an eight-inch Columbiad and two twenty-four-pounder carronades of questionable utility. Still in the yards of John Hughes and Company was the *Livingston*, built sturdily upon a ferryboat hull with three guns, each capable of a wide arc of fire.[12] There was also the privately owned ram *Manassas*, soon to play a major role in Civil War history and in Alex Warley's naval career.

The first mention of the ship's existence came on July 11, 1861, when the Washington newspaper *National Intelligencer* reported to its readers that the Confederate navy was converting a New Orleans tugboat into a steam

ram. Known as the *Enoch Train,* the tug had been constructed in 1855 by
J. O. Curtis of Boston and had a two-cylinder inclined engine made by
Harrison Loring, also of Boston. The cylinders were thirty-six inches in
diameter with a thirty-two-inch stroke driving a single propeller.[13] The
New Orleans privateer *V. H. Ivy* had taken the *Enoch Train* as a prize in
early May 1861. Though the *Enoch Train* is called a packet in one account,
it was described more often as a tug, which is more likely given its power
and structure.

By May 12 Captain John A. Stevenson, secretary of the New Orleans
Pilots Benevolent Association and a commission merchant by trade, had
bought the *Enoch Train* and opened subscription books for investors so he
could raise one hundred thousand dollars to convert it into a first-rate privateer. Privateering had been lucrative in the first month of the war, and
the Confederate government had found itself in competition for shipyard
space and skills with the many private enterprises that were setting out to
create profits on their own. (At least twelve were reported to Union inquiries.) The Confederacy did not pass a law authorizing privateering until
May 21, but Stevenson had been to Montgomery for an interview with
Navy Secretary Stephen Mallory and anticipated that the law would be
passed. Then the Union blockade intervened, essentially putting an end to
Louisiana privateering, and private enterprise in New Orleans drastically
changed.

Stevenson was flexible. Rather than converting the *Enoch Train* into a
fast steamer to take merchant prizes, he decided that his ship should be
remade as a ram to take warships. As a ram, it could earn him 20 percent
of the value of each warship it sank, a good return on investment if it could
sink multiple ships. In an Algiers, Louisiana, shipyard, the *Enoch Train* was
completely rebuilt, adding 15 feet to its overall length (including a reinforced bow with a 20-foot ram) and expanding its beam from 26 to 33 feet.
The new ship was 143 feet long and would draw 17 feet. Displacement was
estimated at 387 tons. The main structure was built with 17-inch-thick
beams with 12-inch oak as primary topside sheathing. Over the oak was a
1½-inch-bar iron layer, not thick by later ironclad standards—and not real
protection from solid shot—but all the weight the structure could bear.
The additional weight was largely responsible for increasing the ship's draft
by more than 4 feet.[14]

Illustrations of the ram drawn at the time—based on observation,
memory, and often sheer imagination—show it as turtle-shaped, often
with one stack. In fact it had two stacks, which were designed to telescope

down for action. Equipped with a spring-shuttered hatch forward for a thirty-two-pound carronade, its pilothouse was aft, behind a lot of things that tended to obscure pilot views. Hatches fore and aft were for access and ventilation. An interesting feature was the pumps installed to eject scalding water over the deck to discourage boarders. Work progressed throughout the summer of 1861 on the ram, first referred to as the "Turtle" but then officially called the *Manassas,* once news of that great victory on July 21 was received. The work was still a private enterprise. When the ship was launched in August, its two-cylinder engine, once thought "powerful," was found insufficient to move about the weight and bulk of the new vessel. The ship was perhaps capable of six knots. In a river that flowed at a speed of between two and a half and four knots, it was indeed limited. New machinery was not an option. The ship was to go with what it had.

While Hollins perceived that his primary threat was from downriver, General Twiggs was firm in his belief that danger came from upriver, where many troops were massing and where Federal timber clads had been under conversion to ironclads in Cincinnati since early summer. Both men had justifiable concerns. Twiggs, however, was confident in the army garrison at Fort Jackson and its older, complementary bastion, Fort St. Philip, directly across the Mississippi at a major bend of the river. Once the bend had been a vital ally of the forts, forcing a sailing vessel to make a major tack upstream while under fire. Steam took away this advantage, working on the side of attackers. Twiggs's perception of danger from the north was legitimate, but his theory was ultimately disproved by the strategy of the Federal fleet.

Hollins had two objectives: defend the city and break the blockade. The second was more immediate and becoming more difficult every day as Federal resources were strengthening at the mouth of the river. The first goal was best termed a "deferred emergency" as no one was currently threatening the city. But the invasion would come and there were two doors to New Orleans.

The current Confederate fleet was clearly insufficient to defend either door, even with Hollins's acquisition of another pair of three-gun revenue cutters, the *Pickens* and the *Morgan,* acquired without Department of Navy approval and in excess of available budget. Navy Secretary Mallory knew of the naval deficiency and, without conferring directly with Commodore Hollins, awarded contracts for building two huge ironclads, the *Mississippi* and the *Louisiana,* to defend the city. Mallory may have been ignorant of General Twiggs's issuance of a contract to construct two large, unpowered floating batteries, the twenty-gun *New Orleans* and the eighteen-gun *Memphis* for upriver defense.

Contracts for the *Mississippi* (260 feet) and *Louisiana* (264 feet) were awarded on September 5 and September 18 respectively—the first to the firm of Nelson and Asa Tift and the second E. C. Murray—with stipulated completion dates of December 15, 1861, and January 25, 1862. Murray was a long-established boatbuilder, originally from Kentucky, who knew a lot about New Orleans and more than most about local supply. Nelson Tift, who owned a plantation in Georgia, had found himself host to brother Asa early in the war, after the Federal navy captured his hometown of Key West and his boat-repair yard. The brothers realized that their new nation required a navy fast and that simplicity was an answer. They designed and built a model of a bare-bones ironclad gunboat and "conceptualized" the *Mississippi*'s details, giving it—among other things—a speed of fourteen knots that would be attained by three eleven-foot propellers, each connected to a high-pressure engine and all powered by sixteen boilers, each thirty feet long.[15]

The *Louisiana*'s contractor, E. C. Murray, developed an inside track, taking immediate options on materials and an existing engine and drive train. Soon the two firms shared a tract of land for adjoining shipyards upriver in Jefferson City, just past Ninemile Point. They developed their facilities while building the craft.

The marine-construction capacity of New Orleans was already full before contracts were awarded for the two monster ironclad ships and the two huge floating batteries. Workmen were scarce; iron had been bought up; machinery could not all be built locally; and the workmen went on strike. Tredegar Iron Works in Richmond remained the only source for propeller shafts of the length needed. Capabilities and supplies had not been researched with any degree of thoroughness before the contracts were awarded. Indeed the order for the two ships seems to have been made in ignorance of the order for the floating batteries. The results were predictable. Delays followed postponements while Hollins waited—and faced other, immediate problems.

9

THE FIRST IRONCLAD IN COMBAT

CSS *Manassas*, October 1861

THE BLOCKADE of New Orleans grew increasingly tighter and was getting closer. The Confederate steamer *Ivy,* a lively 191-foot side-wheel steamer under the aggressive command of Lieutenant Joseph Fry, had been regularly scouting the Head of the Passes and plotting the regularity of the blockaders. It in turn had been observed by Union vessels hoping to capture it. On September 19 the USS *Water Witch* crossed the bar at Pass a l'Outre and steamed to Head of the Passes, running the *Ivy* upstream. Shots were exchanged, and the thirty-two-pounder rifle on the *Ivy*'s stern earned new respect from Lieutenant Francis Winslow of the *Water Witch,* although neither side took damage. Flag Officer William W. McKean, just taking command of the Gulf Blockading Squadron, planned to increase his efficiency by occupying Head of the Passes and building fortifications to block the river at one point instead at the various delta openings.

The *Water Witch,* relatively fast and light of draft, was only the first intrusion. By October 3 the more powerful *Richmond* was at Head of the Passes, as was the *Vincennes,* and the *Preble* was sent over from Ship Island. The inland utility of sailing vessels such as the *Vincennes* and *Preble* was questionable, but they mounted twenty-nine guns between them. On October 5 the *Ivy* found the *Water Witch,* the *Richmond,* and the *Vincennes* at anchor off Pilottown and tried a little gunnery practice with its rifle. Without actually hitting the *Richmond,* Lieutenant Fry succeeded in worrying Captain John Pope, whose nine-inch smoothbores lacked the range of rifles. When the *Ivy* returned five days later, Pope wrote to McKean, "We are entirely at the mercy of the enemy. We are liable to be driven from here at

The Confederate ironclad *Manassas* lying offshore. This depiction shows only one stack, not the two the ship actually had. From U.S. Navy Department, *Official Records of the Union and Confederate Navies*, 1894–1922

any moment, and, situated as we are, our position is untenable. I may be captured at any time by a pitiful little steamer mounting only one gun."[1] This is high praise from the commanding officer of a fourteen-gun, screw sloop—which had been Warley's last U.S. duty station. (The *Ivy* actually had two guns, counting an eight-inch smoothbore, as well as two howitzers.)

The *Ivy*'s success alone could not relieve the problem of the Federal presence at Head of the Passes. Aboard flagship *Calhoun* at New Orleans, Hollins was faced with a problem of numbers. His entire fleet—the *Calhoun*, the *McRae*, the *Jackson*, the *Tuscarora*, the *Pickens*, and the *Ivy*—was essentially outgunned by the *Richmond* alone, gun range notwithstanding. Hollins wanted an equalizer and decided it was the *Manassas*, still in private hands and riding at anchor off Fort St. Philip.

The steam ram's owners, John A. Stevenson and his investors, still hoped to profit by attacking blockaders and using the ship as a privateer. Stevenson had been approached about selling the *Manassas* to the Confederate navy, but the two sides could not come to terms. Hollins, however, was not about to let such a valuable asset go unused when his mission required all the force he could muster.

On October 11, 1861, the *Pickens*, the *Ivy*, and the *McRae* were off Fort Jackson awaiting the arrival of the *Calhoun*, the *Jackson*, and the *Tuscarora*, all of which had left New Orleans on the ninth. The *Manassas* was across the river at Fort St. Philip. Travel time to the forts from the city was twelve to fifteen hours. On Hollins's arrival aboard the flagship *Calhoun*, he wrote the following order: "To Lt Comg A.F. Warley—Sir, You will proceed and take charge of the steamer *Manassas.*" In his narrative, written much later, young Midshipman Morgan gave the account of how this mission was accomplished, beginning aboard the *McRae:*

> To a polite request that it be turned over to us came the reply that we "did not have men enough to take her." The *McRae* was ranged up alongside of her [the *Manassas*] and a boat was lowered. Lieutenant Warley ordered me to accompany him. On arriving alongside of the ram we found her crew lined up on the turtleback, swearing that they would kill the first man who attempted to board her. There was a ladder reaching to the water from the top of her armor to the waterline. Lieutenant Warley, pistol in hand, ordered me to keep the men in the boat until he gave the order for them to join him. Running up the ladder, his face set in grim determination, he caused a sudden panic among the heroic (?) crew of longshoremen who incontinently took to their heels and like so many prairie dogs disappeared down their hole of a hatchway with Mr. Warley after them. He drove them back on deck and then drove them ashore, some of them jumping overboard and swimming for it.[2]

Now thirty-eight years old, Warley had his first command and had to take it at pistol point.

Warley assembled his crew, along with the remaining civilians, and read them his orders. He also broke the news to the civilians that the opportunity for prize money was still good but in a greatly diluted form, as military prize went to all vessels in sight of the capture or destruction, not just the ship directly involved. Fourteen civilians departed, including part owner Stevenson.

Retaining only First Mate Charles Austin, Chief Engineer William H. Hardy, and a local pilot, J. Stevens Mason, from the original crew, Warley assembled volunteers from the various naval commands and commenced on a combination shakedown/combat cruise, not uncommon in the Confederate navy.

Warley had little time to learn the characteristics of the revolutionary craft. He was now commanding the world's first naval ironclad warship to head into combat. It was generally unwieldy, underpowered, and manned by a crew mostly as new to the ironclad as Warley was. He had been up and down the river on the *McRae,* but he would rely on Austin and Mason to pilot the ship. The thirty-two pounder in the bow had limited use and might not be reloadable. The ram appears small in contemporary pictures, but the *Manassas* was 143 feet long. It was a lot of bulk to control with a single screw in a four-knot current on a dark night. The ironclad sat low in the water, with its bow wave washing within two feet of the top of the turtle-back and all that water working against the mostly submerged hull.

Shortly after midnight on the morning of October 12, the little fleet headed downriver. Hollins's operational order put the *Manassas* ahead, to pick the best target for ramming and then to fire three signal rockets to direct the ignition of the three fire rafts that were to be towed into the Federal squadron by tugs. The *Manassas* had been told to attack all targets available. The rest of the fleet would then follow and sweep up the remainder of the forces not rammed or fired.

Not well prepared for the attack, the ships of the Federal squadron were anchored relatively near each other down both sides of the river with the small prize schooner *Frolic* farthest upstream. Next was the sailing sloop *Preble,* then the *Richmond,* almost two hundred yards on its port quarter with the coaling schooner *Joseph H. Toone* alongside. Downriver, off *Richmond*'s starboard quarter, was the steamer *Water Witch.* The sailing sloop *Vincennes* was on the opposite, west bank downstream. There were no pickets upstream, and the night was dark.

Having learned his ship as best he could—the helm, the engine response, and the visual challenge of the aft pilothouse—Warley put on steam and led the way for the twenty dark miles to Head of the Passes. The actual conning of the ship was handled by Austin, who had just been warranted acting master by Commodore Hollins. Austin and Mason knew the river. Slipping into the Federal enclave at 3:40 A.M. with boiler hot but low smoke, Warley tried to see the enemy.

He was almost abeam the *Preble* before he saw it, and the *Preble*'s deck watch spotted him. The *Manassas* swung to the center of the stream to focus on the formation. To starboard was its target, the sloop of war *Richmond.* (In his after-action report, Warley mentioned only that he ran into a sloop of war, possibly not recognizing the ship he had left just ten months before.) "Let her out, Hardy." Warley yelled. "Let her out now!" On the relayed signal from his engineer, the firemen tossed buckets of tar, tallow, and sulphur into the boiler firebox. Swinging to starboard, now in full realization that there was a coaling schooner to miss, the *Manassas* was aimed to the port bow of the *Richmond*. Speed built to what Warley estimated as ten knots. The *Preble*'s crew saw a tremendous plume of smoke belch from the stacks of the *Manassas* as they signaled the *Richmond* and beat to quarters. The first of three broadsides from the *Preble* went above the Manassas.[3]

The prow of the ram penetrated three planks of the *Richmond* some two feet below the waterline, causing a gap of approximately five inches. Warley immediately backed off and looked to the *Preble* as the next target. However, one of the *Manassas*'s engine stages had suffered an upending in the collision with the *Richmond*. Half power at best remained. The ram's next task was to signal upstream for the fire rafts. Opening the after hatch, the midshipman assigned to the task burned his fingers on the match and the first lit rocket escaped into the hull of the *Manassas*, causing a localized panic. He recovered, managing to light and launch three more rockets. As Warley was leaving the scene, the port broadside from the *Richmond* thundered mostly overhead. One of his two stacks was taken out at that time, or perhaps it had been sliced by the hawser between the *Richmond* and coal schooner. As Warley was turning upriver, the flagstaff and second stack were hit, with the stack falling across the wreck of the first one, filling the ship with stack gas. Grabbing an ax, Hardy went on deck over his commanding officer's objections, and, with Austin holding his belt, he cut away the guy wires to the stacks, allowing them to fall away and clear the smoke.[4]

Smoke stacks are built tall not just to take the gases away from the surface; their height creates sufficient negative pressure to allow the boiler discharge to be drawn upward and to pull combustion air into the firebox. Without stacks the *Manassas* had low air flow, low combustion, and low power. On one engine stage and no stacks, the *Manassas* just barely stemmed the current as it headed upstream, away from the Union ships, which had expended some twenty shots in its general direction, but also toward the fire rafts, which were coming downstream.

The *Richmond* had slipped its anchor and headed into the stream to pursue the *Manassas*, but the *Richmond*'s commanding officer, Captain John Pope, then thought better of dealing with the three blazing rafts spread across the river in front of him. He turned tail and headed downstream to the initial amazement of Commander Henry French on the *Preble*, who, on examination of the fire ships, now 150 yards distant, slipped his cable, made sail, and turned his bow downriver.

Lost in the darkness of night and wreathed in his own smoke, Warley was intent on avoiding the fire rafts. Hoping to avoid enemy shot, he turned upstream. When he was free of the smoke, he headed the battered *Manassas* for shore. Grounding was preferable to most other options.

Lieutenant Fry aboard the *Ivy* was extremely relieved to see man and machine emerge from the darkness. He offered to tow the *Manassas* but was refused. The *Ivy* was needed downstream. The *Manassas* might be out of the fight, but it had no need to remove another combatant from the fray. For the rest of the night, the smooth-top "turtle" remained at the shore.

The *Ivy* headed downstream and reached Head of the Passes without encountering an enemy ship. The *Preble*, the *Richmond*, and the *Vincennes* had made their way down Southwest Pass. The *Water Witch*, ignorant of the disposition of the rest of the squadron, had stayed upriver, dodging the fire rafts, which the wind had ultimately carried onto the west bank of the river. By daylight the *Water Witch* observed the other three ships down the pass and proceeded toward them. The immediate mission of its commanding officer, Lieutenant Winslow, was to urge Pope to return upstream to block Pass a l'Outre from the possible escape to sea of the *McRae*, which Winslow had perceived to be a possible blockade-runner or commerce raider. The verbal orders from the flagship, however, were "to get the sloop [the *Vincennes*] over the bar." The first lieutenant of the *Water Witch* was put onboard the *Preble* to assist as pilot. The *Richmond* meantime was determined to anchor and cover the exodus of the sloops.[5]

The *Preble* approached the bar to find the *Vincennes* aground, with its stern upriver and nearly defenseless. Shortly after, the *Preble* felt the sand beneath its keel, but—with two or three smart rolls—she worked off and anchored downstream near the coal ships *Kuhn* and *Nightingale* to provide them protection.

In attempting to turn its head upstream, the *Richmond* grounded, then backed off, but drifted down to ground again. It was now broadside to the current about a quarter mile below the *Vincennes,* which partly blocked the *Richmond*'s otherwise advantageous broadside coverage of the river. The *Richmond* had flown the signal to cross the bar, which at least one of the Confederate steamers mistook as a white flag. It had another meaning for Commander Robert Handy of *Vincennes.* Lodged as he was on the river bar, stern upriver and with limited guns to bear on any adversary, he was vulnerable. He read the "blue-white-blue" signal from *Richmond* as meaning "abandon ship," so he cleared his crew to the boats and set a slow match to the ship's magazine, departing the *Vincennes* about 9:00 A.M.

With some degree of surprise, Captain Pope found the commander, officers, and many of the crew of *Vincennes* scaling the *Richmond*'s rail, Commander Handy with the ensign of his ship wrapped about his midsection.[6] The marine guard and rest of the *Vincennes* crew had proceeded to the *Water Witch*. After the inevitable discussion concerning signals, it was found that not too much damage had been done. The match set to the magazine aboard the *Vincennes* had failed to ignite, and after an appropriate period of time, Pope sent Handy and his crew back to their ship with orders to lighten it enough for it to float across the bar.

This interlude came amid the shelling between the Federal fleet arrayed on and around the bar and the Confederate *Ivy, McRae,* and *Tuscarora,* which had worked itself out of the mud upriver where it had briefly been stuck, not that far from the grounded *Manassas*. Most of the gunnery was at extreme range. Some shots went over the targets. With the exception of some possible shots from the *Ivy* into the stern cabin of the *Vincennes,* no hits were recorded. The total number of attempts, however, was impressive. Lieutenant Fry's clerk recorded a total shot count of *Richmond,* 107; *Water Witch,* 18; *Vincennes,* 16; *Ivy,* 26; *McRae,* 23; and *Tuscarora,* 6. As much as anything, the broadside command of the river by the grounded *Richmond* kept the Confederate flotilla from closing in on the Federal fleet and employing more effective gunnery at closer range. In the Gulf the fifty-gun sailing frigate USS *Santee* tacked back and forth "like a caged lion, unable to get into the fray on account of her great draft."[7]

Between nine and ten in the morning, Commodore Hollins concluded that his little fleet could inflict no more damage or confusion and sounded the recall up to the forts. A tug took the *Manassas* in tow. By the next day the Federals had been pulled off the bar and the blockade, which had been temporarily raised, had been reinstituted. The *Richmond* was on its way to a partial careening for repairs. Captain Pope retired "for reasons of health," and Commander Handy was destined for naval oblivion, the story of the wrap-around ensign following him like an ugly dog.

Hollins and Warley returned to New Orleans as local heroes, having raised the blockade, however briefly.[8] Though Warley had handled the *Manassas* fearlessly, it was demonstrated to be more an instrument of threat than of substance; yet it was valuable in that role. For the ram to return to use in that role, however, much repair was required.

The *Manassas* immediately went into the yards for repair of the extensive damage to the power plant. New engine bracing was designed.

November 6 was election day, but the confirmation of the Confederate government and the actual election of Jefferson Davis was greeted with only muted celebration. The next day the Federal fleet under du Pont took Port Royal Sound, occupied Hilton Head Island, moved swiftly to the town of Beaufort, and established a major base in South Carolina.

Repairs to the *Manassas* took a month or more. Warley used the time getting to know his command and recruiting or training the crew—as best as he could in the shipyards. History does not record the size of the *Manassas* crew at this time; twenty-five to thirty-five men seems likely. There was only one gun to man, an engine room to staff, and the deck and piloting duties to handle. Much of the forward part of the vessel was taken up with solid wood. All survivors of the Head of the Passes engagement were now the most experienced ironclad combat sailors in the world, and many of them had ideas for modification and improvement of their craft. Later, after refitting and training, Warley took thirty-five men down the river to once more meet the Federal fleet.

Warley also spent time crossing the river from the yard in Algiers to the city proper to call on Isabella Huger. Things were progressing well in that department.

There was a continuing conflict of opinion concerning the direction of primary threat to New Orleans. Contrary to the thoughts of Commodore Hollins, the ranking opinion, that of Navy Secretary Mallory, was still that the Federals were coming to New Orleans downriver.

Morale had improved, even if the blockade had not. Now was the time to go upriver and lend support to the Armies of the West. In early December, the flagship *McRae*, now with its topmasts down and secure in its role as a "river steamer" led the *Ivy*, the *Tuscarora*, the *General Polk*, and the *Manassas* upriver to provide support for the new army fortifications at Island Number 10.

Heavy, low-powered vessels heading upriver traveled slowly. Deep-drafted vessels struck many mud banks and usually required assistance in withdrawing. Midshipman Morgan, now aide-de-camp to Commodore Hollins aboard the *McRae*, wrote that "our first disaster happened, when on a dark and foggy night we rammed the plantation of Mr. Jefferson Davis, President of the Confederacy. For this heroic performance, it is needless to say, none of us were promoted, and we lay ingloriously stuck in the mud until we were pulled off by a towboat."[9]

While the body of the fleet was of some assistance at Island Number 10, the *Tuscarora* caught fire and burned off Helena, Arkansas, and the

Manassas was held at Memphis with maintenance problems. Needing more repair facilities than were available locally, Warley spent two thousand dollars of taxpayer money for the steamer *Sertona* to bring the *Manassas* back to New Orleans. They arrived on December 14.

New Orleans lacked command clarity. Major General Mansfield Lovell had replaced the aging Twiggs and found much to do. What he could not do was exercise any control over the naval forces. The Confederate fleet was upriver, and Lovell had an accurate premonition about the intentions of the Federal Gulf fleet, now stockpiling Ship Island. Only two gunboats remained in Lake Pontchartrain. Lovell wrote to the new Confederate secretary of war, Judah P. Benjamin, for help. Almost immediately Benjamin replied with the authorization to seize fourteen local ships, specifying which ones by name. They lacked a lot, but they formed the nucleus for Lovell's own navy. Lovell also demonstrated, to those who were watching, the power of the Confederate army to act and procure as opposed to the navy, which lacked that level of access to the seat of power.

In January 1862 Commodore Hollins forwarded to Warley from Secretary Mallory a letter of commendation for his actions at Head of the Passes. It was nice to have, but Warley would have preferred a promotion. Acutely aware that most of his contemporaries who "stayed north" were close to the commander level, he wrote on February 4 to his cousin William Porcher Miles, now in the Confederate Congress in Richmond: "I hear Bulloch has been made a Captain in the Navy. If it is so it is an outrage on all of us and will cause many resignations at the close of the war. A man who after pursuing his private ends for years being taken up and put over the head of his original seniors who all this time have been in active service is an injustice that high tone men will not bear."[10]

James D. Bulloch, Mallory's emissary to England to arrange ship procurement for the Confederacy, was once a year senior to Warley. The fact that Bulloch was the best man for the job in no way satisfied the Confederate officer corps, who had for all those years in the Union navy served with discomfort and low pay. Bulloch had left active service in 1853 and entered the shipping business in New York. He was in command of the steamer *Bienville* out of New York when word arrived of Fort Sumter. In New Orleans at the time, he was duty bound to return the ship to its owners. Turning down Confederate offers to buy it, he returned the vessel north and journeyed back through his native Georgia to Montgomery to offer his services. He was actually promoted to commander, not captain, to aid in his dealings with British and French authorities.

Congressman William Porcher
Miles, Warley's first cousin.
Courtesy of the South Carolini-
ana Library, University of South
Carolina.

In the his letter to Miles, Warley added, "I suppose you know I am
about to be married. The Lady is a sister of the Miss Huger you met in
Richmond (not the 12 year old tho)." While she was not twelve, she was still
thirteen years Warley's junior. The daughter of Colonel John Middleton
Huger, a planter who had left Charleston in his twenties, made money in
sugar plantations, and served in the Seminole Wars, Belle, as she was called,
was well connected in New Orleans, and at age twenty-five she was a self-
reliant young lady.

Warley also told his cousin, "My 'Ram' is being repaired, her machinery
being attest to compression, I am sorry to say it will be three weeks before
she is ready. When she is I am going to have another dash at the Yankees
and then PROMOTION OR THE BOTTOM OF THE RIVER."[11]

Repairs and acquisitions were progressing. Warley spent thirty-five dollars to have a launch towed in from Fort Livingston, way to the south at the
entrance to Barataria Bay (or Bayou)—considered the back door to New
Orleans—south of the city on the western side of the river. Fort Livingston
mounted a few guns and held three hundred men to guard its shallow-
water approach.

Once again, Hollins led his fleet upriver to counter increased Union activity following the capture of Fort Henry on February 6 and Fort Donaldson on the sixteenth. The *Manassas* was included in the journey upstream but handled badly in the river. Its seventeen-foot draft (increased from its earlier maximum of twelve) handicapped it in a river with a constantly shifting bottom, and its power plant, sturdy enough for the original design, was woefully inadequate for carrying all its solid wood and iron upstream. Below Natchez the steamer *Clara Dolsin* was engaged to tow it the rest of the way to Memphis, where they arrived on March 8, 1862.[12]

On the next day, naval history was revised in Hampton Roads, Virginia, as the USS *Monitor* and the CSS *Virginia* (originally the *Merrimac*) fought the world's first battle between two ironclads. The Union "cheesebox on a raft" fought to a tactical draw with the prototype of the Confederacy's casemate ironclads. Events of the day before, when the *Virginia* slaughtered its wooden rivals without taking damage, demonstrated the dominance of iron. Relatively simple to construct, the casemate design of the *Virginia* was replicated in varying forms in widespread Southern construction sites for the next three years. Hampered by time and shortages of iron and propulsion machinery, many of these ironclads were destroyed before use. A surprising number, however, actually saw combat, sometimes victorious, but never on the open sea. Warley would command two of them.

Without the *Manassas,* the five remaining members of Hollins's fleet headed upriver to New Madrid, Missouri, arriving too late to prevent that town's abandonment. New Madrid was the downstream door to Island Number 10, the last major Confederate block in the river system heading south. At this point the Mississippi becomes confused amid the state of Missouri and the western points of Kentucky and Tennessee. As a twice-bent snake turns back on itself, the Mississippi runs down into Tennessee for a two-mile semicircle, then immediately back north into Kentucky once more, and then back to the south past Missouri into Tennessee. The winding river forms two peninsulas, one pointing south with Island Number 10 at its peak and one pointing north, capped across the water by New Madrid. The distance between the strong points is eleven miles of exceptionally swampy ground.

After several days of heavy Federal shelling with guns that the Southerners had not expected to arrive, the Confederate army and navy both realized that men, equipment, and ships could not survive the pounding. On March 13, the order to evacuate was given. The last shot was fired in return on the seventeenth. With the help of the fleet, the Confederates withdrew, the gunboats moving downstream to Tiptonville.

By March 12 General Lovell in New Orleans was growing increasingly concerned about Federal pressure from the south and requested through General Beauregard that the *Manassas* be sent to him. Hollins's initial reaction was to keep the *Manassas* with him in the event that Union forces would pass Island Number 10. On the fifteenth, however, he wrote Beauregard, "The *Manassas* has been ordered back to New Orleans, as you requested, though from some injury received from a 'snag.' I fear she will be detained some days in Memphis for repair."[13]

The snag incident had broken his propeller, and again Warley authorized spending two thousand dollars for a tow downriver.[14] On the eighteenth the *Manassas* was pulled to dry dock in New Orleans.

Still far upstream, his friend and former commander Thomas Huger wrote to William Porcher Miles in a tone that sounded much like Warley's. Still infuriated over Bulloch's promotion, he wrote that any other navy would have given promotion or some mark of merit to all commanders at Head of the Passes. "The deed of Warley in the 'Manassas' was twice as daring as Buchanan's (though I would be the last to take from that gallant & brilliant feat) for she was the first, an experiment got up in haste and untried, and we all know not invulnerable, we engaged 63 guns with 17 guns in tugboats, towboats and light steamers." He reiterated that serving under a man who left the service at a junior rank and was then promoted over their heads was a mortifying situation. He asked Miles as a friend at home and as a congressman to give "us of the Regular Navy the preference."[15]

Unfortunately for Huger and Warley, the conflict at Head of the Passes sank no invading ships and cleared the threatened area for only a few days, raising the blockade for no more than hours. While medals or promotions have been awarded for valor, they are not difficult to deny in the face of little actual achievement. And Bulloch was doing far more in England than could be expected of him.

The Navy Department was now in Richmond with the rest of the Confederate government. Mallory's prize defensive ships, the *Louisiana* and the *Mississippi,* were not finished. While there was an upstream threat to New Orleans, the downstream menace was greater. Union major general Benjamin Butler, flushed with his success on coastal North Carolina, had taken command of the Department of the Gulf on Ship Island and was building forces for an assault on New Orleans. In December, Mallory had sent

Commander John Mitchell to be commandant of the New Orleans naval station under Commodore Hollins, who commanded afloat. More changes were to come.

By mid-March the command of New Orleans defenses was hopelessly fragmented. With the navy changes, all ordered from Richmond, came Secretary of War Judah Benjamin's move to head the Department of State and an incomplete briefing of the incoming army chief, George W. Randolph. General Lovell—always fighting to retain the troops that were constantly being requisitioned for other theaters—was responsible for the forts and also had to deal with the River Defense Fleet, which he had created. He did not always coordinate with his navy comrades nor they with him.

Lovell had arranged a great chain across the river as a vital component in the defense of Forts St. Philip and Jackson. Buoyed and anchored, it was intended to provide a great obstacle for a force moving against the current and to hold them under the guns of the two masonry forts and possibly subject them to the fury of fire rafts, which would be standing by. Unfortunately by mid-March high water had brought down tons of flotsam, fouling the chain, breaking it, and bogging it down in sections. No heavy chain was available to repair the missing sections and the barricade was patched with hulls of old schooners and rafts. To bolster this more vulnerable barricade, some forty or fifty more fire rafts were built. Whether this information was shared with the navy is not known.

Under the influence, if not command, of Captains Stevenson, James E. Montgomery, and J. H. Townsend, the River Defense Fleet had proved an expensive undertaking of questionable value. The civilian captains—especially Stevenson, still smarting from the loss of the *Manassas*—refused to be placed under the orders of naval officers. More than half a million dollars was still owed the original owners of the vessels. General Lovell despaired of any administrative skills or cooperation among these skippers. As the action developed, almost all they ever did was to get in the way.

With Federal steamers already in the river, peering occasionally at the forts and occupying Pilottown and with the heavy warships of Flag Officer David G. Farragut's fleet struggling to cross the mud bars at the mouths of the river, the powers of defense in New Orleans were becoming increasingly jittery. Captain Whittle telegraphed Hollins, then at Tiptonville, asking that he come downriver.

Hollins immediately took the faster *Ivy*, with the *McRae* following, and headed south. From Tiptonville and again at Baton Rouge, he telegraphed Mallory for permission to bring the rest of his fleet down to the defense of the mouth of the river. His hopes were to take a fleet of gunboats, the *Manassas*, and fire rafts in among the massed Federals and to re-create the confusion that he had caused so well the previous fall. Probability of destroying the invaders was small, but such action would buy time to improve the forts and other defenses, especially the *Louisiana* and the *Mississippi*. Permission never came from the Navy Department, so the rest of the gunboats never descended the river.[16]

The success against Pope that Hollins remembered from the previous October would not automatically have been repeated against Farragut. As his heavier gunboats clambered and bumped and dragged their ways across the Southwest bar at Southwest Pass into the river basin and gathered at Head of the Passes, they received the flag officer's orders on how to prepare each ship against attack. Ships were to be anchored bow on to the current at all times, and one or two guns were to be mounted aft on each poop and forward on the topgallant forecastle. Boat howitzers were to be mounted in the fore and maintops to increase forward firepower, and grapnels were to be kept in ships' boats to tow off fire rafts. Remembering Pope's run, Farragut was precise in instructing his captains that in the event of engine failure and the need to drop down the river, they were to back and fill—that is, manipulate the sails to face upstream while backing downstream—or drop anchor and drift down. In no event were they to turn the ship's head downriver. And, he added, "No vessel must withdraw from battle under any circumstances without the consent of the flag-officer."[17] Things might be different in the face of a downriver attack this time, but the hypothesis was not to be truly tested.

With his ship in the yards and Farragut consolidating downstream, Warley had little time to spare, but he spent what he could with his fiancée. Belle Huger was a child of New Orleans, but a far different New Orleans from the commercially quiet port city, now stripped of its young men and much of its life blood. Towboats sat cold and covered at the wharfs, their machinery giving over to rust. The wharfs had begun to decay from disuse. The only activity along the water was at the shipyards, where work was progressing all too slowly on the ironclads intended to assist the forts in repelling the Federals. The Home Guards units that were drilling in the common areas and squares of the city often comprised the fathers and the uncles, even the grandfathers, of the boys who desperately wanted to be old enough to serve. Nearby the French-speaking Creoles drilled in their dark blue uniforms. The Foreign Legion, men of many nationalities, formed a kind of gendarmerie that relieved many soldiers of their local obligations in order for them to man the forts.[18]

Hard currency was about gone, and Warley, paid in Confederate money, had some buying power, even if it had to be mandated by the city authorities after some merchants (mostly foreign born) had refused to accept any scrip. The problem was compounded with the issuance of money by the state, the city, some banks, and a few drinking establishments. Goods and food were scarce but basic city services were continuing. Schools and courts kept to their routines, and the volunteer fire department was described "as voluntary and as redundantly riotous as ever." News from upriver continued to be bad, culminating in the April 8 news of Albert Sydney Johnston's defeat and death at Shiloh and the fall of Island Number 10, which opened the Ohio River to total Federal control. Porter was moving his mortar boats into position just seventy river miles away. New Orleans life was continuing as usual, but it was about to change.[19]

On March 20, two days after *Manassas* returned to New Orleans, the army succeeded in reworking the barricade across the Mississippi. Without sufficient chain or anchors, schooners were worked into place and anchored, making soft points in the line. Shortly thereafter Federal survey officers were upriver, looking it over and dodging the occasional shot from the forts.

In the midst of preparations to defend the city, Midshipman Morgan entered the office of his commodore to discover that Mallory had summoned Hollins to Richmond in person to account for his conduct. Hollins had acted on his own initiative one too many times for Mallory, who did not fully realize the buildup in the river, the tenacity of Farragut, or the terrible timing of his order.

Hollins's replacement was Captain William C. Whittle, a fifty-seven-year-old Virginian, who arrived with the impression that he was to command the naval station and not the forces afloat. This interpretation of his orders was not completely resolved until later. Commander John K. Mitchell, who under Hollins had been commandant of the naval station, now took command of the *Louisiana*, in the desperate hope of putting it to use. Commander Arthur Sinclair was brought in from his duties of building gunboats in Wilmington, North Carolina, to complete and command the *Mississippi*, still lacking shafts and propellers. Late in the game, Mitchell was given overall afloat command, and Commander Charles F. McIntosh took the *Louisiana*, still not capable of self-propulsion.

The defending forces now included the *McRae* (Huger), the *Manassas* (Warley), the *Louisiana* (McIntosh), the *Jackson* (Lieutenant F. B. Renshaw), and two gunboats of the Louisiana State Navy: the *Governor Moore* (Beverly Kennon) and *General Quitman* (Alexander Grant). Of these commanders, one of the most colorful was Kennon, a former U.S. Navy lieutenant who, as a C.S. Navy lieutenant, did much of the procurement of goods and services under Hollins. The irregularities of budget and overrun (and his affinity for strong drink) caused his resignation from Confederate service and subsequent commissioning as commander in the Provisional Navy of Louisiana State. His was the only ship to sink a Federal warship during the upcoming battle.

His character flaws aside, David Dixon Porter was effective. By March 18 he had crossed the bar with all twenty-one bombardment vessels—a varied lot, each fitted and reinforced for heavy and repeated mortar action. These were towed up Southwest Pass by Porter's four steamers, the *Harriet Lane,* the *Owasco,* the *Westfield,* and the *Clifton.* He then volunteered these steamers to assist the heavy warships across the bar. He sent the *Owasco* upriver for three days to cover the coast survey team, who were to mark the position for each ship of the mortar fleet and provide range and targeting data. Covering seven miles of river, the team laid out the positions to the yard from the forts, giving the lead mortar of the First Division on the west bank a distance of 2,850 yards to Fort Jackson and 3,600 to Fort St. Philip. Six vessels of the Second Division were spotted for a day on the northeast bank, 3,680 yards from Fort Jackson.

Not only did Porter and Farragut have survey information for bombardment, they also had the extensive report of Brigadier General John G. Barnard, then chief engineer for the Army of the Potomac. In the 1840s, along with P. G. T. Beauregard, Barnard was in charge of rebuilding Fort St. Philip and strengthening Fort Jackson. This assignment had given Barnard detailed inside information, some of which was outdated in regard to actual gun counts and recent improvements. The general also proposed a plan of attack, which was considered, while not actually applied.[20]

As the week progressed, the bombardment schooners were towed up and set in their precise places on Good Friday, April 18. Their mastheads had been "adorned" with branches and treetops, and they blended well with the foliage at riverside. The fifteen ships of the First and Third Divisions nestled neatly into the west bank, almost completely invisible from the forts. The six across the river were camouflaged for a while, but soon became obvious, then targeted, and then hit. At sunset Porter assessed his

A mortar schooner firing
into Fort Jackson. From
Century Magazine, *Battles
and Leaders of the Civil
War,* 1887–90.

own damage and, finding little of it on the west bank, pulled the rest to join
them, downstream of the two existing divisions.

Their effectiveness throughout the day against Fort Jackson had been
"deeply cosmetic." While breaching no walls, the thirteen-inch mortar shells
had set a lot of fires and made the parapets untenable. The accuracy of the
Second Division had been superior. They could see the results directly. The
gun crews along the west bank had spotters tied to the mast heads, but by
the time they recovered from the concussion and roll of each shell, they
were enveloped in a black cloud of smoke which may not have cleared until
the shell dropped behind the trees. This happened at intervals of five to fifteen minutes.[21] Spotter duty was exciting but nasty.

Farragut had not placed much faith in the effect of this early bombardment. Most of the old salts expected a few recoils to knock the bottoms out
of their boats, but they did not. and over the next six days, mortar fire at
varying intervals was rained upon Fort Jackson. The damage it did was

extensive but not crippling. Farragut did not appreciate the success of the venture, and observers from both sides disputed its effectiveness after the conflict. Fort St. Philip escaped most of the damage by virtue of its distance.

While the Federal side was organized and effective downstream, reorganization and fraction were blooming upstream. The CSS *Louisiana,* if completed and effective, could have been the plug in the river-chain opening needed to hold up Farragut's fleet under the guns of the forts and turn back the Federals. Technical problems, however, prevented the *Louisiana* from becoming fully operational. The revolutionary and untested propulsion design of two internal paddle wheels in series (one ahead of the other) negated the function of the second wheel and also placed the rudders in their eddy. Steering engines on each quarter were loud but completely ineffective consumers of fuel. When the guns were aboard and mounted, they were found to have such a highly restricted variance in the small gunports as to be virtually untrainable. It did not look as though the propulsion system could be remedied, but as the *Louisiana* was towed downriver from the shipyard on April 19, a full complement of mechanics was correcting all that could be fixed, including mounting the batteries and expanding the gunports.[22] As a sixteen-gun water battery in position of direct cross fire from Fort Jackson, it was considered as the next-most-effective option, even though only the guns on one side could be trained on the enemy at once. It was moored just upstream of Fort St. Philip on the north bank, where it joined the *McRae* and the *Manassas.* Commander Mitchell assumed command of Confederate navy forces afloat and immediately became embroiled in interservice conflict.

Mitchell's immediate problem was Brigadier General Johnson K. Duncan, who was commanding the forts and had his own, legitimate concerns. His supply of gunpowder was finite; his armament was largely smoothbore; the barrier chain across the river was obviously weakened; and he had been pounded upon by twenty mortar boats since the eighteenth. Much of the strain at the main point of impact—the defense of the barrier chain—could be lessened by the placing of the *Louisiana* just above the chain and below the forts. There invading ships would be dealing with a substantial cross fire from a substantial casemate.

This required placement was transmitted to Mitchell, just arrived on the scene, who agreed on the theory of cross fire but who was concerned for the survival of the ship. If but one of the thirteen-inch mortar shells, which had been routinely burying themselves twelve to fifteen feet into the ground before exploding within Fort Jackson, should find a horizontal surface on the *Louisiana*, the strength of its inclined casemate walls would matter little. Work on the ship was incomplete, and the mechanics needed protection. The crew was incomplete as well—and untrained. Mitchell reported these problems to General Duncan on April 22 and followed up by reporting that a conference of his commanding officers had concurred. Duncan acknowledged their concerns but with the reservations of a man who really needed that cross fire.[23]

No less a challenge were the half-dozen adventurers in the River Defense Fleet. On April 20 Mitchell had been put in command of this army-financed collection of armed steamers. Carrying one or two thirty-two-pound pivots and faced with flat iron across the bows for ramming, they protected their machinery to some degree with double pine barricades and sheltered the crews against canister behind compressed cotton. If each steamer could be counted on to ram one upcoming gunboat, perhaps the Federals could be held in front of the forts and pounded by the heavy guns ashore. Unfortunately the steamers could not be relied on for anything. The day after he was put in charge of this "fleet," Mitchell received a letter from John Stevenson, calling himself "Senior Captain, Commanding River Fleet at Fort Jackson":

> Sir: I am receipt of an order from Major-General M. Lovell, dated 20th instant, in which I am directed to place myself and my whole command at this point under your orders. Every officer and man on the river-defense expedition joined it with the condition that it was to be independent of the Navy, and that it would not be governed by the regulations of the Navy, or be commanded by naval officers. In the face of the enemy I will not say more. I will cooperate with you and do nothing without your approbation, and will endeavor to carry out your wishes to the best of my ability, but in my own way as to the details and the handling of my boats. But I expect the vessels under my charge to remain as a separate command. All orders for their movements addressed to me will be promptly executed, if practicable, and I undertake to be responsible for their efficiency when required. I suppose this is all that is intended by the order of Major-General Lovell, or that will be expected from me by you.

In a postscript, Stevenson referred to coordinating signals and graciously concluded, "Anything I can do, rely on it being done promptly and cheerfully."[24]

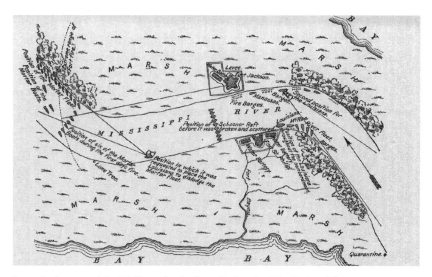

Forts Jackson and St. Philip a day before the battle. The Federal fleet came
upstream from the left. From U.S. Navy Department, *Official Records of the
Union and Confederate Navies,* 1894–1922.

Two days later, on April 23, the eve of the battle, Mitchell forwarded the
letter to General Duncan, explaining that Stevenson had so qualified the
navy's authority as to relieve Mitchell of all responsibility for the River
Defense Fleet. He did, however, include Stevenson in a conference that
afternoon with his commanders.

Many fire rafts had been constructed, mostly by the army, with the
intent of pushing them down the river into the upcoming Federal forces.
Some were intended to be sent down individually, to light up the river
night and just to "worry" the Federal fleet. Some previous raft attempts
with Stevenson's force had not gone well, and the rafts had eddied out near
Fort Jackson and illuminated only its shore. One had even burned one of
the hulks in the river barricade and opened a hole in center stream. Stevenson was again detailed to send down the rafts, one with each steamer, when
the Federals were due to come upriver.

Also on the twenty-third, General Duncan told Mitchell that an enemy
boat had planted a series of white markers on the Fort St. Philip side and
that the Federal attack was anticipated. "Please keep the river well lit up with
the fire rafts tonight," asked Duncan.[25] Mitchell detailed launch number six

to maintain a bonfire and to stand by below Fort St. Philip with rockets and a howitzer to warn of movement, but no fire rafts went downriver. On all the Confederate ships, steam was up and a ready watch was alert but no more so than on most of the previous few evenings.

The situation on the evening of the April, 23, 1862, was a good case study in eve of battle. The Federal forces were powerful and well organized. Farragut had a firm hand over all his ships and people and knew his plan. He was to run his fleet (seventeen ships mounting 192 guns) up the passage through the chain, pass the forts in the minimum possible time, and move directly to New Orleans. Some of the power of the forts, especially Jackson, had been reduced by days of unrelenting mortar pounding. Porter took credit for this, but was disappointed when the forts were not completely reduced by bombardment alone. Farragut, who had accepted the mortar fleet as a possibly desirable add-on, was now convinced that he was right in not expecting that fleet to totally eliminate the forts. Porter, however, was opposed to his superior's (and adoptive brother's) plan. Running directly to the city would leave a powerful enemy at the rear of the fleet and possibly endanger Porter's flotilla. The plan would place Porter far to the rear when the city surrendered. He would find it difficult to maintain the credit and glory that was his by desire if not by right. Yet, minor in-fighting aside, the United States Navy was ready.

Confederate forces lacked several components of readiness. Armies and navies had not yet worked together on the North American continent, and the Confederate battle plan was not to be the shining introduction of combined operations. The army owned the forts and the chain. The competence of their gunners was spotty; artillery pieces were fewer than what the fort could hold, and their numbers were reduced daily by Federal mortars. Duncan had also ended up with nominal responsibility for the River Defense Fleet. Navy Secretary Mallory had made a bad call on the immediate threat and changed commanders too late in the game. John Mitchell was a good officer, but he had just arrived on the scene and had little local knowledge. Captain Whittle back in New Orleans had his job prodding the construction of the ironclads and left afloat matters to Mitchell, now at the forts. Mitchell's assets included a powerful and untested floating battery, a steam ram of much reputation and limited effectiveness, two navy gunboats with a total of nine guns, two Louisiana gunboats with a total of four guns, three launches with one howitzer each, and seven small unarmed steamers and tugs, used as tenders, messengers, and fire-raft tenders. With the chain this little force had to hold the Federals under the forts long enough for the big guns to eliminate them or force their withdrawal. The Confederate naval force's confidence in the chain was less than General Duncan's. In a joint defense conference a few days earlier, the general had discussed its integrity, and, knowing Farragut's reputation, Warley had remarked, "General, if I commanded a fleet below and my commission lay above your obstructions, I would *come up and get it.*"[26]

10

A Short Night and
a Long Morning

The Battle of New Orleans, April 1862

The stillness of a huge river at night is baffling. All is painted in varying shades of black, and the water is moving but seems still. Alex Warley was lying in his bunk on *Manassas,* not quite asleep in the way of most commanding officers and fully dressed. The spring had not yet run to hot weather, and no one intends to go to his hour of glory in his pajamas. At 3:30 A.M. his executive officer, Lieutenant F. M. Harris, awakened him with the news that there was activity at the chains. No warning had been given. On seeing movement in the enemy fleet, Acting Master C. B. Fairbanks had brought launch number six, the warning launch, upriver to near Fort St. Philip and headed into the swamp. The River Defense Fleet had not sent down the fire rafts. There were no rockets, no warning, and no illumination.

Steam was up on the *Manassas,* and on Captain James Brown's little tug, the *Phoenix,* which was just inshore. The *Phoenix* pushed the bow of the *Manassas* out into the river, giving Warley a good heading on his day's first target, the USS *Cayuga.* Then the River Defense ram *Resolute,* fleeing upriver, ran directly into him. As the *Manassas* backed away to clear itself, the *Cayuga* poured a broadside into the *Resolute* and continued upriver.

Warley still had other targets and stood down toward the USS *Pensacola,* but he was too late, passing just under its quarter and causing no damage. He then made for a "large sidewheel steamer," not recognizing his old home the USS *Mississippi,* and struck it on the quarter as the larger

April 24, 1862: The Federal fleet is shown moving across the chains between Fort St. Philip (on the near bank) and Fort Jackson. The *Manassas* (depicted with a single stack) is shown maneuvering to ram the *Mississippi* (third in line) as Farragut's division is moving up the far bank, firing on Fort Jackson. The ships at center right are some of the schooners that held the chain in place. The unfinished CSS *Louisiana*, moored at Fort St. Philip, is at the bottom. From Century Magazine, *Battles and Leaders of the Civil War*, 1887–90.

vessel was swinging to avoid the *Manassas*, bringing the two alongside. Lieutenant George Dewey, at the helm of the *Mississippi*, discharged a broadside, which passed above the *Manassas*, and then headed upstream. Damage to the *Mississippi* had been impressive, but not mortal. A section of solid planking seven feet long, four feet broad, and four inches deep was torn out. The collision "nipped off the heads of fifty copper bolts as clean as if they were hair under a razor's edge." In the course of dealing with the *Manassas*, the *Mississippi* had been under the guns of St. Philip. Ten shots hitting the vessel, with eight going completely through. Warley was attempting to hold the Federals under the guns of the forts. Soon he found himself at the forts and under their guns himself. This was not in his plan. Realizing that most of the Federal fleet had passed him, he considered working downstream to destroy as much of the Federal mortar fleet as he could. In range of the forts and taking several hits from his side, he realized that one hit from a seven-inch or larger gun would be final. He beat back

upriver to discover a ship-rigged vessel lying across the stream. This was
the USS *Brooklyn*, partially grounded and not moving. Almost any steer-
ageway (sufficient motion to allow steering) qualified a ship to outrun the
Manassas, but here was a stationary target. Warley threw on all steam and
struck "fairly amidships," firing the carronade just before impact. The
collision knocked the gun off its slide, disabling it for the duration, and
knocked everyone on the *Manassas*, except the helmsman, off his feet.
Chain "armor" had been draped over the side of the *Brooklyn*, and the
ramming had driven chain into the planking but had failed to penetrate.
Days later, when investigating unusual leakage, the *Brooklyn*'s carpenters
discovered five feet of planking stove in and severe structural damage. Only
a full coal bunker had prevented a major hull penetration.[1]

Backing free, Warley cast about for another target. As dawn broke, he
spotted the *Iroquois*, the thirteenth ship in the Union line, and set up an
approach to ram it, but the Federal ship put on steam and left the *Manassas* behind as if it were at anchor. Two more ships—one of which may have
been the *Pinola*—sent broadsides in his direction, making at least six ships,
plus the forts, to blast him.

In the emerging daylight, moving upstream toward the quarantine station above the forts and just downstream of the city, Warley saw the *McRae*
in combat with four gunboats at short range. Knowing that his gun was
disabled, his hull holed forward and amidships, and his ramming capability compromised by riddled stacks, Warley was also aware that his presence
was far more impressive than his actual threat. He made for the fray to give
some relief to the *McRae*, whose commander, his friend Thomas Huger
was dying, and allowed it to fall back under the forts. Two of the ten or
twelve Federal ships (as counted by the pilot) came down the river, the *Iroquois* on one bank and the *Mississippi* on the other.

Taking stock of his resources and options, Warley determined that he
had done all he could to resist the enemy's passing the forts—indeed he felt
he had been the only Confederate vessel at the forts—and his duty now was
to save those under his command. He had not enough room to turn and
head downstream, and his chances of outrunning the *Iroquois* and the *Mississippi* were negligible anyway. He headed toward the east bank, taking a
bead on the *Mississippi*, which sheared away. With sufficient momentum to
hit the shore, Warley had the steam-delivery pipes cut, and the *Manassas*
nosed into the bank where it sloped up steeply.

As the Federal warships ranged alongside and poured grapeshot into
the shore, Warley ordered his crew out through the bow hatch into the

Lieutenant Thomas B.
Huger in his Confederate
naval uniform. From
J. Thomas Scharf, *History
of the Confederate States
Navy*, 1887.

swamp. He and Harris followed them. Lying low for an hour and a half of grape fire, they finally outlasted the problem and reassembled with some survivors from Fort St. Philip. After the Federals had moved toward New Orleans, they found a boat and crossed the river. Heading upriver on the western bank levee, they heard that the *Louisiana* was still afloat and flying Mitchell's pennant. Warley turned back downstream and joined his commodore.[2]

Warley and the *Manassas* have been described as "being almost everywhere." There were other actions of note but few at the point of action, under the forts. The dark and the smoke held up the USS *Pensacola* and the USS *Mississippi* for a time. The USS *Varuna*, originally fifth in line, broke through and worked its way upriver to meet the Louisiana Navy's *Governor Moore*. Its captain, Beverly Kennon, had it moored to the bank with *Manassas* when the action began, and Warley told him to "follow us." Kennon's report indicates that, while trying to get off the bank, he was fouled by at least five Confederate river and other steamers, and finally ran into to the *Belle Algerine* to "rid myself of [its] annoying presence."[3] The action between the *Varuna* and the *Governor Moore* upriver, near quarantine station, was spirited and deadly, involving the sinking of both. Kennon fired through his own bow to hit the *Varuna* and then repeatedly rammed it, aided some by a ramming from the River Defense Fleet steamer *R. J. Breck-inridge,* commanded by Captain James B. Smith. Observing the rest of the Federal fleet steaming upriver toward him, Smith then considered his job done and headed for the bank, where he set fire to his vessel and retired ashore.

Thomas Huger had taken *McRae* to just upstream of the forts and attempted to hold back the invasion. He exchanged broadsides with most of the First Division and reaped the unfortunate results one would expect from an encounter between a converted merchantman and a half-dozen men-of-war. After temporarily grounding to fight a fire in his sail locker, he was backing away from the shore when the *McRae* was shelled by more passersby. He was mortally wounded by a shell fragment. New lieutenant "Savez" Read took command and headed upriver to find himself in the fix that Warley attempted to alleviate with his last actions afloat.

The River Defense Fleet came in for well-deserved criticism. Some of their actions were indefensible; all were uncoordinated. Exceptions, such as Smith's one action against *Varuna,* also include Stevenson's taking the *Warrior* into the fray at the forts and attempting to ram and board the *Brooklyn* just before its encounter with the *Manassas.* A progressive shrapnel broadside from the *Brooklyn* (with one-second fuses) ended the attempt. The *Warrior* grounded on the eastern shore and was set afire.[4]

It was not the Confederate navy, independent rams, or the chain that held up the invaders at the river bend. It was the current, darkness, and smoke. Collisions, temporary groundings, and disorientation placed Bailey's First Division where it was not supposed to be. Then Farragut took his Second Division right into the tangle. The Federals gathered off the quarantine station late that morning with fourteen of the original seventeen ships. (The *Varuna* was there, broken and beached.) They dealt with their 36 killed and 135 wounded and speculated on the fates of the *Itasca,* the *Winona,* and the *Kennebec,* which did not make it past the forts. The surviving thirteen moved up to an anchorage eight miles below the batteries at English Turn and spent the night. By early afternoon on the next day, the twenty-fifth, they arrived at New Orleans in a driving rain in time to watch the Confederate ironclad *Mississippi,* as powerful an unfinished man-of-war as they had ever seen, float by them with flame and smoke issuing from every opening. It had been fired in the shipyard and cast away.

The CSS *Louisiana* was immobile as a ship and, as a battery, it was half misapplied. Tethered to the bank just upstream of Fort St. Philip, in its original position, with only six of its sixteen guns applicable, it was a factor in the battle, but not the decision maker that the Confederates had hoped and the Federals had feared. In the smoke and dark, the *Louisiana had* failed to fire on some of the early Union vessels, including the *Katahdin,* which used its eleven-inch gun and forward pivot to hull the ironclad forward and dent the casemate iron. Commander McIntosh was observing topside, where he was severely wounded by splinters from the sharpshooter barricade and soon died. Left in the wake of the Federal fleet—in company with the barely serviceable *McRae* and the two damaged forts—she was the remainder of Confederate navy presence and was the rallying point for whatever Confederates were left on the afternoon of April 24.

Reporting to Mitchell and paying his respects to the dying McIntosh, Warley became the senior serviceable former commanding officer available for council to the commodore. He was there the next day when the mortar barrage resumed and on the twenty-sixth, when Porter packed up and sent his mortar fleet down to Head of the Passes. Porter's offer to receive the surrender of the forts had been termed "inadmissible" by Duncan on the afternoon of the twenty-fourth.

On the twenty-seventh, however, the beat-upon, burned-out, and demoralized garrison at Fort Jackson—who faced Federals upriver, Federals downriver, and Butler's Federal troops working the back doors through the swamps—staged a mutiny, changing the complexion of the army's future at the bend in the river. A flag of truce was sent out the next day from Fort Jackson with a proposal to accept terms, and General Duncan and Colonel Higgins made their way aboard the *Harriet Lane* to sit down with David Porter.

From the start Porter could tell that the Confederate army, as represented before him, had little use for its own navy.[5] This observation stemmed from Duncan's request and Mitchell's refusal to position the *Louisiana* at the chains in Federal mortar range. Duncan was convinced that he was at this juncture because the *Louisiana* did not hold Farragut in front of the forts. He had some reason to believe this. There were also anecdotes of gunner inefficiencies, such as the Louisiana backcountry artillery captain who continuously depressed his muzzle to hit close-in ships, and the enthusiastic run out of his gun caused the shot to roll out the barrel into the moat. When told that his cannon fire was all sound and useless fury, he steadied himself and concentrated his fire on one ship, which unfortunately proved to be part of the Confederate chain across the river.

On the positive side, Federal ships sustained in excess of 120 hits, many serious, and three ships had not passed the obstacles. The small fleet had

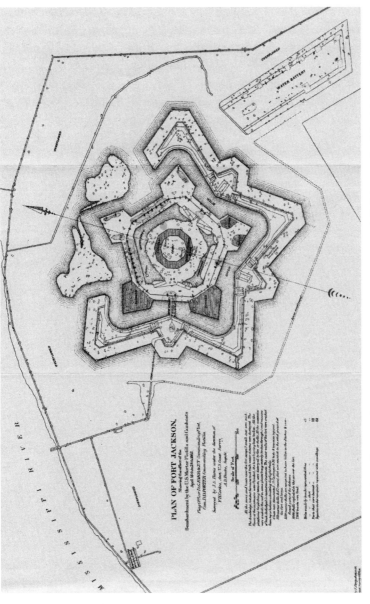

Postaction damage plan of Fort Jackson. From U.S. Navy Department, *Official Records of the Union and Confederate Navies*, 1894–1922.

done much of the serious damage. Some fire rafts, one or two steamboat rams, and the *Manassas* had all contributed to the confusion of current, smoke, and dark in the collisions at the barrier, but the lack of coordination and the position of the *Louisiana* stood out in the minds of the army, who had lost their strength and with it New Orleans. The army line was that it was surrendering the forts and the land forces but not the ships and that the army "had nothing to do with the Naval Officers and were in no way responsible for their acts." As the terms of surrender were being presented, the results of a recent Confederate navy council of war were unfolding just upstream. Commander Mitchell had called Lieutenants Commanding Warley and Wilkinson (now of the *Louisiana*), and Lieutenants Ward, Whittle, Bowen, Arnold, Harris, and Shyrock for advice. Warley was senior among the afloat commands and recommended setting fire to the *Louisiana* to keep it out of Federal hands. Porter was already considering its value as a Federal floating battery, which could be towed to Mobile or up the East Coast.[6]

It was decided to act on Warley's suggestion immediately, with a solid attempt to flood its magazine and neutralize the ten thousand pounds of powder aboard. This magazine had not been designed for flooding, however, and there was a lot of dry powder remaining.

As a decent gesture, Captain Whittle's son Lieutenant W. C. Whittle Jr. was sent to the *Harriet Lane* to inform Porter that the *Louisiana* had been fired and could constitute a hazard to the U.S. forces then under a flag of truce. The ironclad was then moored about three quarters of a mile from the nearest Federal vessel. By the time Whittle had procured a boat and was nearly at the *Harriet Lane*, the *Louisiana* had burned through its moorings and was about a ship's length from its position on the bank. Its guns began to cook off, and the magazine exploded, throwing iron in all directions. The only casualty was a man on the parapet of Fort St. Philip. As soon as he could and with trepidation over his timing, Whittle boarded the *Harriet Lane*.

After a fifteen minute wait for the commander to emerge from a meeting, Whittle delivered the warning message to Porter, who replied, "Say to Captain Mitchell I am much obliged to him." Porter's courteous reply was lost in events. He began to realize the loss to the United States of the *Louisiana*. His subsequent reports resulted in much discomfort for Mitchell, Warley, and the other Confederate naval personnel. As the ironclad was set afire, Mitchell and his remaining staff boarded two remaining small steamers and headed upstream, with no thought of escape. Lieutenant

Commanding Jonathan M. Wainwright brought the *Harriet Lane* up to the steamers and fired a shot, halting them. They hove to and dropped their colors. Wainwright, by now infused with the delayed anger of his commodore, told Mitchell "that if he had not supposed the transport to contain wounded men he would not have come alongside, but would have poured broadsides into her until she sank." Instead he took aboard fourteen naval officers—including Warley—and seven engineers, who were transferred to USS *Clifton* as prisoners of war.[7]

The more Porter dwelled on how capture of the *Louisiana* could have added to his achievements and the progress of the Union fortunes on the Gulf, the less he remembered that the Confederate army actions did not involve navy actions. He began to feel that the setting afire of the ironclad, while Porter was sitting under the army flag of truce was treacherous, bordering on barbarism. This was the impression he conveyed to Farragut, who acted accordingly.

All former U.S. Navy officers aboard the USS *Clifton,* a one-year-old converted New York ferryboat, were held under close confinement. They were allowed on deck only twice a day for "indispensable visits." Hot spring weather was making itself known to these prisoners, and they were still not completely aware why their treatment was so harsh, especially when compared to the treatment of officers from the fort, most of whom had been paroled. Warley noticed that his brother officers of the old service had not given him a friendly word or hardly a glance when they recognized him.

Unknown to these captives, immediately after the conflict, Lieutenant Read had been granted leave to take the *McRae,* full of wounded, upstream for medical assistance in New Orleans with the condition that he would return the vessel to the Federal fleet. The *McRae,* however, sank in its moorings at the city when the crew could not keep up the pumping necessary to keep it afloat. Perhaps the crew would not keep up the pumping required to return the ship to its captors. Regardless of what caused the sinking, Read could not find any logic in returning the remainder of his crew to enemy hands without the vessel. He went upstream with other evacuees and stayed free to fight again. While in the Confederate view the *McRae* was "sunk," the Federal view was that it had been "scuttled," adding to Porter's negative impression of the opposition.

Reporting to Farragut on his capture of the Confederate officers the following day, Porter referred to the burning of the *Louisiana:* "I made them surrender unconditionally, and for their infamous conduct in trying to blow us up while under a flag of truce, I ordered them to close confinement as prisoners of war, and think they should be sent to the north and kept in close confinement there until the war is over, or they should be tried for their base conduct."[8]

Porter's report to Gideon Welles on April 30, two days after the action, displays a continuing increase in personal anger toward the situation that had denied him the prize of the CSS *Louisiana*. He no longer seemed to remember that the conditions of surrender applied only to the Confederate army. In his report to Welles, Porter went on to say:

> Seeing her lying so quiet, with colors down and the two steamers lying under our guns, I never dreamed for a moment they had not surrendered. [Mitchell] failed to cooperate like a man with his military confederates, who looked to the means he had at his disposal to save them from destruction and who scorned alike his want of courage in not assisting them, as well as the unheard-of and perfidious act which might in a measure have reflected on them. How different was the course of the military commanders, who though engaged in so bad a cause, behaved honorably to the end. Every article in the fort was delivered up undamaged: nothing was destroyed either before the capitulation or while the capitulation was going on, or afterward.[9]

There are obviously different ways to look at this situation. Besides the loss of *Louisiana* to the U.S. Navy, the immediate result of its destruction was the discomfort of the Confederate prisoners, described by Commander Mitchell from the after berth of the *Clifton* on May 1, when he wrote to Flag Officer Farragut asking him to understand that the *Louisiana* was destroyed while the navy was under no flag of truce and requesting appropriate conditions for prisoners of war. Farragut's reply, written six days later, took Porter's description of events as gospel, citing also the "scuttling" of the *McRae* as further evidence of Confederate "regardlessness of the rules of civilized warfare" and reiterating the order that Mitchell's command be "made close prisoners and sent to the North to be dealt with by the Government as it may deem proper." A concurrent message to Commander S. D. Trenchard, commanding the side-wheel supply ship USS *Rhode Island* (to which the prisoners had been transferred) directed him to "treat the rebel officers as prisoners of war and according to the manner in which they may conduct themselves. I do not wish them to be treated with too much harshness, nor with too much consideration."[10]

The stay aboard *Clifton* had lasted only until May 5, when the coal and supply schooner USS *Fearnot* took the prisoners from Pilottown out to the frigate *Colorado* in the Gulf, where they were transferred to *Rhode Island* four days later. From that time, according to Mitchell's letter to Secretary Welles, conditions improved. There was no improvement, though, for Commander Beverly Kennon of the Louisiana Navy, whom Mitchell found aboard the *Rhode Island.* As a former U.S. Navy officer, without a Confederate navy commission, he was accused of abandoning his men on *Governor Moore* and was "seen" throwing a wounded steward overboard as the ship was sinking. Kennon later told his version, explaining that the steward was wearing a life jacket, the water was shallow, and the ship was on fire, but he did not have an opportunity to explain at this time. Kennon was confined on "very grave charges," the exact nature of which were unknown to Mitchell or even to Kennon. The day after the Confederate officers boarded the *Rhode Island,* the ship stopped by Ship Island, then sailed to Pensacola, whose naval base had recently been evacuated and largely destroyed by its departing defenders, and then went to Key West on the fourteenth. A week later they stopped in Hampton Roads, and on May 23, the *Rhode Island* discharged its prisoners at Fort Warren in Boston Harbor.[11]

On landing at Fort Warren, the officers signed an agreement not to take advantage of the relative freedom of the prison fort.[12] This arrangement was almost immediately modified by a directive from the U.S. Navy Department that had been sent from Washington the day before.

Two days into formal confinement at the fort, Commander Mitchell wrote to Navy Secretary Welles that he and Lieutenants Wilkinson, Warley, Ward, Whittle, and Harris "have been denied the privileges and courtesies that are extended to other prisoners in the fort on the grounds that destruction of *Louisiana* was 'infamous.'" He enclosed a letter from Lieutenant Whittle explaining the nature of his visit to warn Porter and the others in the surrender conference of the danger posed by the burning ironclad. By return mail four days later, came a reply from the secretary to Colonel Justin Dimick, commander of the fort, accepting Mitchell's explanation and lifting the restrictions on "John Mitchell and his associates." (Welles still refused to refer to Confederate rank in his dealings with the prisoners.) He stated, however, "This does not relieve Beverly Kennon from the restrictions imposed on him." After another three weeks of local requests, Mitchell again wrote to Welles asking for a copy of the "very grave charges" against Kennon. Welles reply was to Kennon, asking for the "particulars of the destruction of the gunboat under your command." In his reply detailing the events, Kennon also mentioned the lack of rank and forms of address in Welles's letters. On July 3 Welles directed Colonel Dimick to remove all restrictions on "Mr. Beverly Kennon."[13]

With more or less the run of the island, the twenty-eight officers from the Battle of New Orleans passed the months of June and July. They were in good company. All the officers captured at Fort Donaldson were there as well as those members of the Maryland legislature and Baltimore city council who had been arrested for treason. Many of the prisoners had family, business, or social connections in Boston, and these individuals assisted in the prisoners' provisioning and comfort. Even without connections, the prisoners had access by daily tug to the markets of Boston and could provide for the general mess in addition to standard army rations. Colonel Dimick was almost less a jailer than a landlord. He was invited to some of the messes of his "guests" and enjoyed their high regard. When Dimick's son was ordered to active service, there was a near-unanimous prayer from the prisoners that he be spared from suffering or death. The weather was better in the North too, and their friends knew where they were. Sarah Morgan, sister of Midshipman Jimmy Morgan, entered in her diary, "Brave Capt. Warley, that dare devil, is prisoner on his way to Ft. Warren, the home of all brave and patriotic men. We'll have him out. I wish I could fight for him."[14]

Warley was exchanged on July 31, 1862, for Captain Alfred Gibbs of the Third U.S. Cavalry. A steamer took him to Aikens Landing, Virginia, on August 5. Two days later, he received back pay in the amount of $1,124.36, after affirming that he had been a Lieutenant Commanding until his exchange on the fifth.[15] He was brought around to Fort Monroe, opposite Norfolk and then up the James River past Harrison's Landing, where McClellan's huge army was crouching, foiled in its attempt to take Richmond during the Seven Days' Battles. Aikens Landing was about twenty-five miles down the snakelike James from Drewry's Bluff, the major Confederate base defending Richmond. There the exchanged prisoners were met and processed home by naval personnel, including some of the many midshipmen stationed there. These included Jimmy Morgan, who had found his way to Richmond after the fall of New Orleans.[16]

11

Back to South Carolina

CSS *Palmetto State*, August 1862

As HE HAD DONE SO OFTEN, Warley returned to Pendleton, where he wrote a version of his battle as a letter to the editor of the *Pendleton Courier*.[1] When the Federals had occupied New Orleans, Belle, his intended, had relocated inland with her family to Jackson, Mississippi. Major General Benjamin Butler, who had commanded the land forces just behind Farragut's fleet, was now running New Orleans, where he soon earned more than nicknames. "Spoons Butler" had some connection to the personal wealth with which he left the army after the war, and "Beast" concerned his personal dealings with the populace. A few surviving New Orleans porcelain chamber pots have his image adorning the target area.

After almost three weeks at home, Warley, now somewhat of a hero, received orders to Charleston from the Bureau of Orders and Details, signed by its chief, his late wife's father. Captain Forrest may have sent for Warley as a favor, but more likely he was responding to a request by Captain Duncan Ingraham, Warley's old mentor. Ingraham commanded Naval Station Charleston, and Warley was detailed as first lieutenant of the new ironclad *Palmetto State*, still under construction.[2] Buoyed by the news of the Confederate army's victory at Second Manassas, Warley left Pendleton on September 1, arriving in Charleston the next day. His first order of business was acquiring new uniforms. What had not been lost aboard the *Manassas* had been ruined in swamps and prison. Also everyone else in Charleston was wearing gray, and that finally included the Confederate navy.

He was lucky to find gray cloth for his uniforms. Commodities were becoming scarce in the South although some goods were coming through

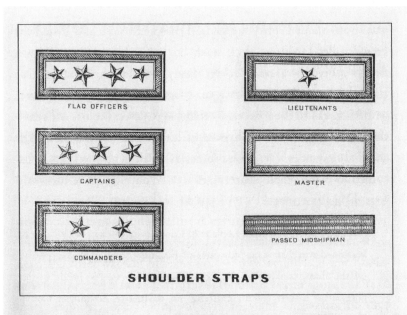

SHOULDER STRAPS

FLAG OFFICERS

LIEUTENANTS

CAPTAINS

MASTER

COMMANDERS

PASSED MIDSHIPMAN

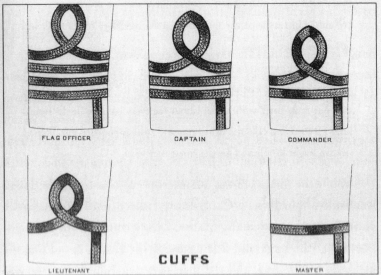

CUFFS

FLAG OFFICER

CAPTAIN

COMMANDER

LIEUTENANT

MASTER

Above and following pages: Confederate naval officers' insignia and uniforms

FLAG OFFICER

LIEUTENANT

CAPTAIN

MASTER

COMMANDER

PASSED MIDSHIPMAN

CAP ORNAMENTS

SURGEON OF OVER 12 YEARS

PASS^d ASS^t SURGEON

SURGEON OF UNDER 12 YEARS

ASS^t SURGEON

MEDIUM

LARGE

SMALL

CAP ORNAMENTS
& BUTTONS

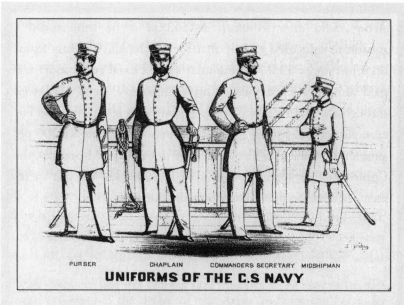

PURSER   CHAPLAIN   COMMANDERS SECRETARY MIDSHIPMAN

UNIFORMS OF THE C.S NAVY

FLAG OFFICER   CAPTAIN   LIEUTENANT   SURGEON

UNIFORMS OF THE C.S NAVY

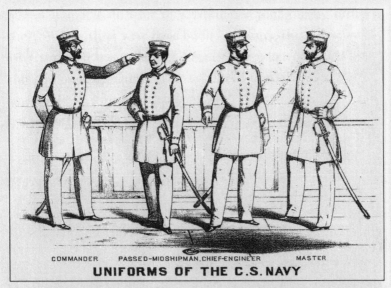

COMMANDER   PASSED-MIDSHIPMAN, CHIEF-ENGINEER   MASTER

UNIFORMS OF THE C.S. NAVY

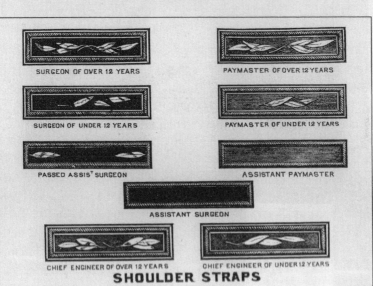

SURGEON OF OVER 12 YEARS   PAYMASTER OF OVER 12 YEARS

SURGEON OF UNDER 12 YEARS   PAYMASTER OF UNDER 12 YEARS

PASSED ASSIS⟂ SURGEON   ASSISTANT PAYMASTER

ASSISTANT SURGEON

CHIEF ENGINEER OF OVER 12 YEARS   CHIEF ENGINEER OF UNDER 12 YEARS

SHOULDER STRAPS

the blockade in Charleston and some of the shipments were always designated for the locals by local blockade-running captains. Captain Smith Lee, then commanding in Richmond, had already ordered his steamers not to keep steam up when not actually on duty. Boilers were to be cleaned every ten days, as much an efficiency measure as a performance enhancer. Further, he told his skippers, "you will haul down your colors on the near approach of a squall and hoist them again when the squall is over as bunting cannot be had."[3] Ingraham was not as far inland as Lee, but he was also feeling the pinch.

The brief career of the *Virginia/Merrimac* earlier that year had proved that the basic slope-sided casemate design for ironclads best fit the needs of the South. The *Merrimac* was a U.S. Navy steam frigate rebuilt, but the new "look-alikes" were constructed from the keel up. Straightforward in construction, not requiring extra machinery (as for turrets), and capable of surviving punishment, the profile lent itself to a smaller hull, generally 150 feet in length and the new Richmond Class was replicated across the South. The *Palmetto State* was one of these ships and had the main fault of the entire class: inadequate propulsion.

The ironclad mounted an eighty-pounder rifle forward, a sixty-pounder rifle aft, and an eight-inch shell gun on each side. The fore and aft rifles could pivot 180 degrees to three available ports, allowing a broadside of three guns at a time. Four inches of iron covered the twenty-two inches of heavy wood siding on the casemate. The engine was from another craft and drove the vessel up to seven knots, all conditions being favorable.[4]

A fellow South Carolinian, Lieutenant John Rutledge, had command. First Lieutenant Warley had the direct problems of manning and provisioning. He also had to oversee completion of the ship's construction on the ways of Marsh and Sons at the foot of Market Street on the Cooper River. Such work was always a challenge. Although laid down in January, it lagged well behind its sister ship, the *Chicora,* which was started in April and launched in August. Whether it was the Confederate financing for the *Palmetto State* versus the South Carolina backing for *Chicora* that made the difference (in Charleston) or greater industry by the neighboring Eason Shipyard may never be decided, but delays in transportation and acquiring timber and iron plagued both shipyards. By late September, Warley was writing to his friend Robert Minor, "God knows when we will be ready." Even when the *Palmetto State* was ready, the ways were not. Two thousand pounds of mud were drained and dragged off the river bottom to allow the ironclad to slip down into the water and float.[5]

The original funding for a "gunboat" had been much encouraged by women's organizations. Because 15 percent of the cost of the *Palmetto State* was raised through donations, fairs, and bazaars, it was known as one of the "ladies' gunboats" funded in part by women residing in several major cities of the South.[6]

Finally by October 11, with all available dignitaries on hand and the *Chicora* already in midstream and "fully dressed," the *Palmetto State* was launched. The two ironclads, Charleston's Harbor Defense Fleet, were afloat. By November they were operational as a squadron, but they were never really ready for offshore combat. Their motive power was so weak that the *Chicora* once had to anchor in the channel to keep the tide from overwhelming its propulsion and taking it out to sea.[7]

This was Warley's second posting to Charleston, and it was not to be his last. He found the city changed since his time on Morris Island in the spring of 1861. He was staying at perhaps the finest hotel in town, the Mills House, which had survived the December 1861 fire that had ravaged 540 acres of the city and consumed 575 homes and many businesses. The most distinguished guest at the Mills House during the conflagration had been General Robert E. Lee, who watched most of the late evening fire from the hotel's roof and then carried a baby away from the building to assist some ladies in their escape. Dedicated employees had draped wet carpets over the balconies and out the windows on the side facing the fire to save the building from the fate of its neighbors.[8]

Also in Charleston in late summer was Midshipman Jimmy Morgan, recently arrived from Richmond and assigned to the *Chicora*. The sixteen-year-old knew no one in town except Warley and "the great difference in our rank, as well as age, precluded the possibility of my making a companion of him." Morgan remained alone for a time until joined by another young mid, George Hollins, son of his old commodore. Being assigned to ships under construction and having little or no money, they shared a room in a fourth-rate boardinghouse until early September, when young Hollins was stricken with yellow fever, which was rampant in Charleston that summer. In only two days time Hollins—racked with fever and covered in vomit—died in Morgan's arms. Morgan went in search of Lieutenant Warley, who told him not to worry about Hollins's funeral as "Mr. Trenholm would make all the arrangements." In the meantime Warley directed the young man to come and share his room at the Mills House. A few days after the funeral, the two were walking home down Broad Street and met "Mr. Trenholm," who invited the youngster to come and live at his

Midshipman James Morris "Jimmy" Morgan at age fifteen. From James Morris Morgan, *Recollections of a Rebel Reefer*, 1917.

house for the time being. The young Louisianan politely declined. A couple of days later they met again and again the invitation was extended with the addition, "Warley, I am sorry this young gentleman won't accept my invitation, I would try to make it pleasant for him." Warley turned and said, "Youngster, you pack your bag and go up to Mr. Trenholm's house."[9]

Thus Morgan found himself virtually the ward of one of Charleston's wealthiest and most influential shippers and businessmen. George A. Trenholm, a partner in three of the South's largest shipping firms, was largely financing the Confederacy and was destined to be secretary of the treasury —and Jimmy Morgan's father-in-law. One of Trenholm's business partners in the Charleston firm of John Fraser and Company was Warley's brother-in-law, Theodore D. Wagner. Through his newfound connections, Morgan went to England and then cruising aboard the CSS *Georgia*. Warley finished the launching and outfitting of the *Palmetto State* and assisted

George A. Trenholm.
Library of Congress.

in underway trials and formulating two-ship operations in Charleston Harbor.[10]

Alex Warley had another mission, one that was overdue. He journeyed to Jackson, Mississippi, where on December 1, 1862, he married Isabella Middleton Huger. He brought her back to Pendleton. After a honeymoon severely restricted by the surroundings of war—and by the remoteness of Pendleton, South Carolina—he returned to Charleston. Later that month the Navy Department sent him orders to testify in Richmond at a Court of Inquiry concerning the fall of New Orleans. He reported on January 5, and immediately his travel calendar filled up. The combination of his service record and the influence of his first father-in-law, who was still heading the Bureau of Orders and Details, presented him the opportunity to put to sea on a raider—the best possible assignment.

As shown by John Maffitt on the *Florida* and Raphael Semmes on the *Sumter* and the *Alabama*, commerce raiding was glamorous, potentially profitable, and often an avenue to promotion. It was also increasingly difficult to get started as a raider. The raiders were usually obtained overseas; ships were in short supply; and getting there involved running the Federal blockade.

The USS *Harriet Lane* had been captured by the Confederate army in a New Year's 1863 attack conceived and executed by Major General "Prince John" B. Magruder, using two cotton-clad vessels in his recapture of Galveston, the only Federal foothold in Texas. Magruder's bold action had destroyed the USS *Westfield*, recovered the city, captured more than six hundred prisoners, and acquired a potential commerce raider. Not wishing to lose this opportunity, the Navy Department took possession of the prize and immediately began assembling a crew. Lieutenant J. N. Barney was given command, and Warley, five years his junior, was given orders on January 10 to report to him in Galveston. Barney was good, proven in previous conflict, and he was happy to have Warley.

The prospective executive officer returned immediately to Charleston, packed his sea bag and took out a one-hundred-dollar per month allotment for his family in care of Theodore Wagner, an attorney as well as a businessman. Granted advance travel pay by Commodore Ingraham, Warley headed west on January 15.

Just getting to Galveston was a challenge. The South Carolina Railroad took him through Branchville to Augusta, Georgia, where he changed to the Georgia Railroad and traveled to Atlanta, where he observed that new commerce center. He then changed to the Atlanta & West Point line, which became the Montgomery & West Point on the way to Montgomery, Alabama. All this travel was at ten miles per hour. Track maintenance took precious resources, and slow speeds saved wear and tear. At Montgomery he boarded a riverboat to Selma, where the Alabama & Mississippi Rivers Railroad took him to Meridian. A change to the Southern Mississippi Line got him to Vicksburg, and the optimistically named Vicksburg, Shreveport and Texas took him to its western terminus at Monroe, Louisiana. Working his way to Shreveport on horseback, he then traveled by rail on a few miles of track to Marshall, Texas, on a line destined one day to go to El Paso. By stagecoach and horseback he made the long haul from Marshall to Nacogdoches, Huntsville, and Houston, finally boarding the Galveston & Houston cars for the last fifty miles to the coast. His travel pay had been based on a total distance of 1,619 miles to Austin, as the paymaster in Charleston was "unable to arrive at a distance to Galveston." It had taken him three weeks.[11]

Barney had been in place two days before Warley's arrival and was not impressed with the ship. Familiar with the intensity of army-navy conflict in the debacle of New Orleans and well aware that the *Harriet Lane* had been taken by the army, he was walking delicately with General Magruder, who in turn was being gracious while holding superior rank and the high ground of having captured the vessel now appropriated by the navy. When the vessel had been lightened to get over the bar into Galveston Bay, it had lost all its armament, most stores, even masts, "everything but her engine."[12]

While assembling a crew, Barney's first task was to evaluate the *Harriet Lane* as a cruiser. From best guesses and talks with its former engineer, now a prisoner, Barney concluded that it could carry about six-days' coal and would do some eleven knots under steam and sail and five to seven knots under steam alone. It had run out of coal between Washington and Key West.

The *Harriet Lane* was described as being fast in smooth water, but it could make but little way in a head sea—wind and sea coming from ahead (over the bow). If it could not succeed as a raider, Barney was of the opinion that a navy crew would be a waste and an affront to its original liberators.[13] Magruder wanted the ship mostly for harbor defense, and it was agreed that mixed leadership of forces afloat, which had done so poorly in the recent past, would not likely do much better here.

In the meantime Barney's first lieutenant had made his own evaluation and was not impressed with the opportunities afforded by a dismasted, disarmed, bay-bound brigantine. Warley requested a transfer. Barney reminded him that he had been posted to Lieutenant Barney and not to the ship. The orders had been worded that way to preserve the confidentiality of the possible cruiser, but, Barney said, he could not just release Warley. Both officers, however, had concluded that the Confederate oceangoing future of the *Harriet Lane* was shaky, even if it could initially get through the Gulf Coast blockade.[14] By March 9 it was clear that Barney wanted to ship out on a cruiser, but the *Harriet Lane* was not a fit cruiser, and Magruder wished the ship fitted out only so far as required for its own self-defense. Warley was detached on the tenth with instructions to determine the state of protective obstructions at the head of Galveston Bay on his way home and to telegraph back to Barney. He was to carry dispatches to Richmond in a condition that would allow them to be destroyed to prevent their capture. In the same arduous means of travel by which he arrived, he returned to the East Coast, this time going to Richmond, which took eighteen days.

Warley then received orders to become Ingraham's executive officer in Charleston. Signing the orders this time was the new chief of the Bureau of Orders and Details, Commander John K. Mitchell, Warley's afloat commander in the brief but tumultuous time in New Orleans.

Posting to a naval station with an active squadron is an opportunity for command. Available positions come up suddenly. Even as he was unpacking his bags at his hotel in Richmond, tired of riding trains that he could (for a short distance) outrun, the USS *Isaac Smith,* emboldened by its apparent invincibility in repeated forays up the Stono River just south of Charleston was caught in a web of Confederate artillery cross fire. The Stono enters the ocean at the south end of Morris Island after meandering southward between Johns Island on the west and James Island on the east. On January 28 two batteries of the First South Carolina Artillery had been brought overland and hidden in positions on Johns Island and just beyond, on Thomas Grimball's plantation. Two days later, in broad daylight the *Isaac Smith* steamed up the Stono, almost catching the ambushers by surprise but passing the first battery without detecting it. As soon as the vessel anchored, it came under fire from the second. Casting loose, it headed downstream into the lower battery and a hail of musketry, which swept its decks even as three twelve-pound shot took out its boiler. Unwilling to fire the ship because of the casualties, the captain surrendered with eight dead and seventeen wounded. The *Isaac Smith* entered the Charleston Squadron as the CSS *Stono* that afternoon, but it took four hard days to get it through the low water on the land side of the island and more time for repairs.[15]

An army capture of a 171-foot ship with nine guns was an event indeed, but not the last of the day. After midnight, the two Confederate ironclads slipped out past Fort Sumter, intent on damaging the blockading fleet. Commodore Ingraham had his flag on *Palmetto State,* whose captain, John Rutledge, had taken his friend Lieutenant William Harwar Parker as his executive officer on Warley's departure. The *Chicora* was commanded by Captain John R. Tucker, whose first lieutenant, George H. Bier, had complained that he had not expected to see much action as long as "old Ingraham" was in charge. "Tucker would be better,"[16] he felt.

Passing the forts and steaming along Morris Island in Main Ship Channel, the two ships—and 260 men, some asleep—approached the bar about four in the morning and then went silently to battle stations. The *Palmetto State* rammed the USS *Mercedita* and the *Chicora* made for USS *Keystone State.* Both Federal vessels sustained initial, crippling damage, which caused both to haul down their colors. Reassessment of their situations and the inability of the Southern ships to out steam even a crippled seagoing vessel, however, allowed both Federal ships to raise their flags again and move out. Accounts from each side presented differing points of view and charges of breach of honor. However, both damaged vessels remained with their own fleet, sustaining twenty-five killed and twenty-two wounded. Parker was told years afterward that the crew of the *Mercedita* actually had considered themselves captured (although their ship was not), observed their parole properly, did not communicate with other Federal vessels, and were regularly exchanged the following April. This might be considered "honor of no consequence."

The rest of the blockading fleet, being constructed of wood, backed off from the ironclad invaders and retreated to the south. The Confederates spent the night off Sullivan's Island until the tide allowed them back across the bar. They observed the Federals, hull down to the south but with masts still visible in the long glass, and the Confederate crews remained skeptical when Beauregard and Ingraham announced sufficient victory to declare the blockade "raised." The ironclads returned to port, where their crews were gratified at the public attention but aware that more could have been done. The twenty-four-hour period of the engagement was a good one for Confederate arms in the lowcountry. Unfortunately for Charleston, however, as the ironclads returned to harbor, the blockaders returned to position and resumed the cordon about the port.

Alex Warley reported to his "station of opportunity" on April 6, cursing his luck at missing the only action involving the ironclad he had left to go to Galveston. The next day the action resumed when Rear Admiral Samuel F. du Pont launched his major attack on Fort Sumter and Charleston Harbor. It was yet another battle in which Warley played no role.

Du Pont, now commander in chief of the South Atlantic Blockading Squadron, had taken Port Royal, South Carolina, and cruised into Fernandina, Florida. The darling of the U.S. Navy Department since long before the war, he was now, however, running afoul of Navy Secretary Gideon Welles and Assistant Secretary Gustavus Fox, who wanted Charleston and were sending him monitors—a class of flatdecked, turreted ironclads named after the famous original *Monitor*—in total confidence that they were the key to its automatic capture. So impressed were they with the performance of the original *Monitor* at Hampton Roads, that they assumed it would be omnipotent against all other ships in any situation. So optimistic were they, that they saw the reduction of Charleston as a strictly navy venture and victory.[17] Du Pont saw otherwise but said too little. As a result his reputation as a fighter began to suffer.

P. T. G. Beauregard and his predecessors had not been idle in the defense of Charleston Harbor. Constantly working to strengthen the outer defenses of Forts Sumter and Moultrie, he had added to the inner-harbor fortifications of Castle Pinckney, Fort Johnson, Morris Island, and White Point Gardens (the Battery). The city's defenders were prepared to fight street by street if necessary.

The Confederate submarine service had been established to apply the newly pioneered underwater torpedoes and old-fashioned physical ob-structions—poles and rocks—in the channels. Nets and cables added to the tangle. The primary strategy was to hold attacking ships under the guns of the forts. This plan was easier to implement in Charleston than it had been at New Orleans.

The Federal fleet gathered outside the harbor on the afternoon of April 6, 1863, with the monitors and the ironclad frigate *New Ironsides,* du Pont's flagship, anchoring inside the bar. During the night a blockade-runner came up the main channel and into the harbor unchallenged. Because the anchored vessels were inside the bar, the blockade-runner had thought they were Confederate. To counter the Northern preparations, the forts had gone to full alert, and the *Palmetto State* and the *Chicora* had left their pier. As part of the inner ring of defense, they had taken up their pre-arranged station off Fort Johnson.

At one o'clock in the afternoon, the monitors moved in behind the *Weehawken,* pushing an Ericson-designed minesweep bow attachment. Fort Moultrie opened fire at 2:50 P.M. with the other batteries joining in as range allowed. From then until 4:30, when du Pont made the signal to recall, and then until 5:25, when the fleet withdrew from range, the nine ironclads had endured 2,209 shots and 520 hits,[18] a tremendous pounding. The *New Ironsides,* in the middle of the line, was hit 50 times from Fort Moultrie but with no armor penetrations. Du Pont's flagship had run aground, however, and was forced to anchor generally out of the fray near Sullivan's Island.

This accidental anchorage was directly over a large, electrically activated mine under the charge of Confederate assistant engineer Langdon Cheves, who had the opportunity of a lifetime and no success. Whatever he did to the electrical circuit, the mine did not explode. The wiring was traced out in the possibility that a wagon might have run over and severed the leads in the sand, but they found no breaks. For an hour Cheves agonized, even while du Pont sat by in defeat as his ships took concentrated fire from all fortifications. Cheves's court-martial eventually concluded that the mine failed because the wiring was too long for the available battery power.

The USS *Keokuk* was in a sinking condition, and another four of the eight Federal monitors were in "disabled" condition when the recall was sounded. Both sides considered the day a "reconnaissance in force" until the Union commanders assembled that night aboard the *New Ironsides,* withdrawn offshore with the blockading fleet, and confessed the amount of damage to their ships. Du Pont cancelled the expected renewal of battle for the next day and "saved a defeat from becoming a disaster." Loss of life was limited to one in the fleet and two in the forts, with few wounded on either side. Damage to the forts was generally cosmetic, in a masonry sort of way. The Confederate squadron, limited to steaming in circles near Fort Johnson on the south side of the harbor, had an excellent view but no part in the action. They remained on station, expecting a Federal return, for the next three days.[19] Warley had a view from the wharf on the Cooper River.

The U.S. Navy Department laid blame for the defeat squarely on Admiral du Pont. His relief was Rear Admiral John A. Dahlgren, a man well-known for his development of ordnance and all too eager to have a fleet command. Du Pont returned to Washington, never again accepting permanent orders, but serving on various boards until his death from a bronchial attack in 1865.

"Promotion or the bottom of the river," Warley had declared to his cousin. He had tried. He had the reputation of being a fighter, and his former father-in-law had fostered what opportunities were available. By virtue of "going South" at the start of the war, he had reduced his options from many to few. If he had remained in the U.S. Navy, he would have been a lieutenant commander (or better) by this time, and with the ever-expanding Federal fleet, he would have had a chance at making captain. Even David Porter—hardly generous with praise for his rivals, let alone his adversaries—referred to Warley as, "a gallant young officer, formerly of the old service," after the battle below New Orleans.[20] But not following South Carolina would have pitted Warley against his home state and against his grain. With so many others, he found himself in an ever-narrowing tunnel of opportunities, with ships being destroyed and ports being taken. More ships than officers were being lost. Here Warley was in Charleston, a spectator to a conflict that all the C.S. Navy merely watched, and he was available.

Nonetheless life in Charleston was eventful. The Federals were bombarding the city. There was little human habitation south of Broad Street. In the months of April and May 1863 in spite of the blockade, more than

The Mills House Hotel in 1865. The finest hotel in Charleston, this building survived the great fire of 1861, when General Robert E. Lee was a guest there, and was Warley's residence during his tours in Charleston. It was completely rebuilt in the 1970s. Library of Congress.

ten thousand bales of cotton departed in twenty-one ships, made it past the Federal fleet, and headed toward the English mills that were clamoring for it. Fifteen blockade-runners made it into the harbor. Brigadier General Quincy Gilmore, fresh from his conquest of Fort Pulaski, near Savannah, had taken over the Union land troops around Charleston and was pushing up the rivers and creeks, preparing for an invasion of Morris Island. Gilmore's strategy was to move from the narrow southern end of Morris Island, take Fort Wagner, and use the north end of the island as a base from which to bombard Fort Sumter into submission, as he had done to Fort Pulaski from Tybee Island. Beauregard had anticipated this strategy and was convinced that giving up all Morris Island would result in damage to Fort Sumter, but that he would not lose it. He was right, and Morris Island would not be given up easily.

On May 15 unusual, direct orders from Navy Secretary Mallory gave Warley command of the repaired CSS *Stono*, instructing him to run the blockade to Nassau with cotton and bring back sheet steel.[21] Warley lost another chance for glory, however, because as the orders arrived, he and General Beauregard were involved in testifying at the army's court of inquiry into the loss of New Orleans.

Convened at the request of Major General Mansfield Lovell, the court had met in early April in Vicksburg, then reconvened in Jackson, Mississippi, and again in Charleston, finally adjourning on July 13. Lieutenant Warley reconfirmed what he had said all along, that to have anchored the *Louisiana* within range of Porter's mortar boats would have been suicide. He stated that they seemed to have the range to hit his *Manassas*, for "at the explosion of the first shell I hauled out of my position, but had not removed a ship's length before two mortar shells fell in the position I had held, and I subsequently counted 60 shots that struck within a short time the place the *Manassas* had retired from." The final decision was that General Lovell was not at fault.

While Warley was at the court of inquiry, the *Stono* was preparing for its maiden run but not under him. Instead he had orders to Richmond, and from there he took leave to Pendleton. As he was leaving for Richmond, the *Stono*, under Lieutenant James H. Rochelle, departed on the night of June 5, encountered the blockading fleet, and returned. Closing too near to Sullivan's Island, the *Stono* washed up on the breakwater near Fort Moultrie. It was severely damaged. Its cargo was salvaged, but the recovery of the ship and repairs took months.[22]

Warley spent almost a month helping at home. There was still time for planting and always a shortage of labor and management to get it done. In early July the navy sent him orders to report to Flag Officer J. R. Tucker for duty aboard the *Chicora*. Tucker had recently taken command of Charleston's forces afloat in a move to remove operational command from the elderly and entrust it to men more inclined to action. Ingraham retained command of the naval station in Charleston. Tucker directed Warley to "take charge and assume the duties of Lieutenant Commanding, CSS *Chicora*."

The Confederate ironclad *Chicora* in Charleston Harbor. From James Morris
Morgan, *Recollections of a Rebel Reefer*, 1917.

Three weeks later, on August 5, Warley led a raiding party of four boats
and thirty men of the Twenty-fifth Regiment, South Carolina Volunteers,
under Captain M. H. Sellers, to the north entrance of Light House Creek.
Federal observers had been moving in and out of here with regularity, and
Beauregard had said it must stop. Captain Sellers landed with some of the
men as two boats went around to the mouth of St. Vincent's Creek to cut
off the enemy's barges. "A brisk skirmish ensued, which resulted in the capture of one boat with one captain and ten non-commissioned officers and
privates of which the captain and four others were wounded, one mortally." The night was a total Southern success. As usual Warley was profuse
in the praise of his compatriots, specifically lauding Captain Sellers and his
men for "their strict adherence to directions and gallant dash in finding the
enemy."[23] Unknown to Warley, his brother Felix, a wounded artillery major,
had been captured the night before in a small boat that was transporting
him to Charleston. The Federal launch that picked up Felix Warley compromised the element of surprise in its real mission, which was an attack
on Battery Gregg at the tip of Morris Island. The attack failed, but Felix
remained a prisoner of war.

Flag Officer Tucker warmly endorsed Warley's report of his raid to
Secretary Mallory, who responded with a fine letter of commendation, but

again no promotion. Not many Confederate naval officers had been promoted for valor.

Summer in Charleston rolls on interminably until late September, by
which time the citizens of Charleston are usually exhausted by the heat and
humidity. In peacetime those with the means to flee to higher ground left
the city for the upcountry, the mountains, or at least to Summerville, just
twenty miles inland, where fevers were not as likely to strike. In wartime
many citizens in the lowcountry had been burned or bombed out and had
moved permanently away, many to the state capital in Columbia. Those
remaining, especially men in uniform, remained busy. The nearby Federals in blue uniforms remained busy also. The summer of 1863 was filled
with raids, skirmishes, experiments with new weaponry, and some serious
conflict. The main Federal efforts were aimed at Morris Island, the key to
Fort Sumter, the harbor, and the city. Union troops moved onto the south
end of Morris Island in heavy fighting on July 9, and on the eighteenth, in
conjunction with the guns of the Federal fleet, they assaulted Fort Wagner
in what was one of the most compactly bloody and gallant efforts of the
war. General Beauregard and even the Charleston newspapers praised the
heroism of the enemy attackers. With the failure of the assault, Gilmore settled in siege warfare, with constant assistance by heavy guns of the blockading fleet. (See the map of Charleston harbor on page 67.)

Life in the harbor fleet was monotonous and uncomfortable. Baking in
the sun, the ironclads rotated picket duty and were required to have an officer on deck at all times, in port or out. Because of shortages on manpower
the assistant engineers were pressed into service to help with deck watches.
By law they were not required to stand watch, and a corrective letter from
John Mitchell, now commander in charge of the Bureau of Orders and
Details, pointed this out to Flag Officer Tucker.

Boat raids were ongoing, as were plans to attack the blockaders with
spar torpedoes in launches. As commanding officer of the *Chicora,* Warley
supported one on August 22, if only to provide bacon, bread, and sugar.
He also provided the first volunteer officers and crew for the experimental
submarine *H. L. Hunley.* Lieutenant John A. Payne, as commanding officer
and Lieutenant Charles H. Hasker led five men from the *Chicora* and one
from the *Palmetto State.*[24] This crew swamped the *Hunley* off Fort Johnson,
drowning five of the men and taking Hasker twenty-four feet to the bottom before he could release his foot from the forward hatch cover. He was
one of four crew members who survived. The *Hunley* made history the

next year, sinking USS *Housatonic* before sinking itself and carrying to the bottom its entire third crew.

Fort Wagner on the north end of Morris Island was under siege, receiving endless heavy-caliber pounding from shore and sea. The Federal artillery had established the Marsh Battery on James Island and its famous Swamp Angel, a 16,300-pound Parrott cannon, lobbed shells into Charleston proper until the huge gun burst from the repeated heavy charges required to handle the range. The defenders of Fort Wagner had less and less to work with as their own guns were disabled by incoming rounds. The decision to evacuate was finally made on September 5, ending fifty-seven days of defense under most difficult conditions. The next night forty boats were sent to the north end of the island with steamers standing by as close as possible to receive the men from the small craft. Only a skeleton crew was left behind to keep up a deceptive fire, spike the remaining guns, and blow up anything worthwhile.[25]

Federal barges appeared around Cummings Point and fired on the Confederate evacuation launches with their boat howitzers—ultimately capturing two, carrying nineteen seamen and twenty-seven soldiers—but the evacuation was considered a success. "One of the most delicate [operations] ever attempted in war," wrote Beauregard.[26]

Throughout the summer the *Palmetto State* and the *Chicora* alternated days in the channel opposite Fort Sumter, as the first floating line of defense. Fort Sumter was under fire and was reduced to an infantry command with a single fieldpiece and two hundred troops. The day following the evacuation of Morris Island, Admiral Dahlgren summoned Sumter to surrender. The response was, "Come and take it."[27] Since they had not recently received artillery shot from the fort, Dahlgren and General Gillmore assumed that only infantrymen were defending the now almost-shapeless pile and that it could be taken by a large force of small boats. A landing force of almost five hundred Federal sailors and marines was assembled for an attack on September 8.

At two o'clock in the afternoon of the eighth, the *Chicora* had picket duty in the channel, and Lieutenant Clarence Stanton had the deck. His signalman turned to him and announced that "Fort Sumter will be attacked tonight." "How do you know?" asked Stanton, and the signalman answered, "I have just read their signals."[28] The Confederates had broken the Federal codes, and the signals people knew them well. Stanton passed to the Confederate commodore the information that each ship in the Federal

Charleston Bay and City, by John Gadsby Chapman, showing the *Chicora* and the *Charleston* with Castle Pinckney on the right. Courtesy of the Museum of the Confederacy, Richmond, Virginia.

blockading squadron was to send one boat to assemble at the flagship at ten that night. Flag Officer Tucker alerted the garrisons of Forts Moultrie and Johnson, on opposite sides of Sumter, and the *Chicora*, instructing them all not to spring their trap until Federals walked into it. Once the Federal boats reached the beach at Fort Sumter and landed their assault team, the *Chicora* poured in canister and grapeshot while Forts Moultrie and Johnson hit both flanks with solid shot and shell. Sumter's defenders were shooting down at the enemy, as well as throwing hand grenades and even loose bricks, of which there were many. The Federals moved up against the walls for what shelter they could find and soon surrendered. Only three of their number were killed in the process. More than one hundred became prisoners.

A subsequent Confederate army-navy contest over who should claim the captured launches was won by the navy after they found that the only launch damage was made by canister, and Warley's *Chicora* was the only supplier of canister that day.[29]

Soon after this battle, Warley turned over the *Chicora,* and he was back in Pendleton in October. By the end of the month, he had received orders making him Flag Officer Ingraham's "number one lieutenant" once more. Warley was not as likely to organize individual raids now, as Lieutenant James Rochelle had come back to town with a force of 130 officers and men to organize all available small craft for harbor defense and transportation. All boats not previously spoken for now belonged to Rochelle.

Warley's commissioned status had changed too, along with that of most of his contemporaries. On May 1, 1863, President Davis had signed a law establishing the Provisional Navy of the Confederate States.[30] Conceived by Secretary Mallory, the law came upon the heels of separating commands afloat from the station commands ashore—a move to help control the very senior men. Malory had learned this problem from the law of April 1862, which provided for the limited promotion opportunities for "gallant or meritorious conduct during the war." In his files were protests from senior commodores French Forrest, Arthur Sinclair, Ebenezer Farand, Robert Pegram, and others who considered this move injurious to the best interests of the service. The older captains had a claim by seniority on the operational jobs. They were as offended by the concept as Warley and Huger had been when Bulloch was promoted above them. The junior officers, however, eagerly welcomed these promotion opportunities.

The Provisional Navy was a navy within the Confederate navy. There was no mention of it in the navy secretary's report to President Davis in November 1863, but the end of April 1864 report indicated that it had been organized and formed. A general order of June 2, 1864, transferred all enlisted men, petty officers, and up through the warrant ranks into the Provisional Navy. Selected commissioned officers down through midshipmen were transferred at that time. Raphael Semmes, now second senior captain in the new list, wrote to say that the younger and more active men were culled out and placed in the Provisional Navy, leaving the regular navy a "kind of retired list" which still included bureau chiefs, station commanders, and commanding officers of yards and ordnance facilities.[31] Warley made the cut, ranking ninth among first lieutenants in the Provisional Navy.

With the siege in its second year, Charleston had developed a siege mentality. Bombardment had slowed, except for the little garrison in Sumter, who were regularly pounded. Naval security was tightened. Flag Officer Tucker directed that all ship's boats were to be alongside their ships and hoisted out of the water by sunset. If this were not practical, the oars were to be taken out and stored below. All officers and men were to be aboard by sunset. For a while in September, all liberty was cancelled to limit communication during a yellow-fever epidemic. As a naval station officer, Warley lived in town and continued to walk to work. He received "commutation of quarters and fuel" at the rate of two hundred dollars per month, which in Confederate dollars, was not much money.[32]

12

Two More Commands

CSS *Water Witch* and CSS *Albemarle*, 1864

IN LATE SPRING of 1864, Commodore W. W. Hunter, commanding the Savannah Squadron, appealed to Captain Smith Lee at Bureau of Orders and Details for officers to man his steamers. The ironclad *Savannah* was not yet commissioned, but most available manpower in the area was already assigned to that ship. Hunter needed officers to run his little steamers *Isondiga* and *Ogeechee*, in part to disperse their crews from the baking oven of the *Savannah*, in which they were housed. He asked Lee for an additional three lieutenants, a master or passed midshipman, and four midshipmen, even more if the *Water Witch* should be commissioned, which it was soon to be.

The USS *Water Witch* had been taken in Ossabaw Sound, just south of the mouth of the Savannah River, on June 3, 1864, by a boarding force commanded by Lieutenant Thomas P. Pelot and 125 sailors and marines. Pelot lost his life early in the boarding. The ship was taken up the Vernon River with hopes of taking it through the Skidaway River into the Savannah River just downstream of Fort Jackson and seven miles above Fort Pulaski, which was in Federal hands. Though they lightened the ship as much as possible, the could not bring the *Water Witch* any farther up than White Bluff on the Vernon River. In the middle of summer, this disarmed and disabled ship in a marsh was Alexander Warley's new command.

On June 28, he reported to the Confederate States Prize Steamer *Water Witch* in White Bluff, Georgia, approximately ten miles from the city of Savannah, having spent forty dollars for a carriage ride to transport him and his baggage. Prospects for career-enhancing action were not good. The *Water Witch* was stripped of everything that increased its draft. It was left with two boats, one anchor and chain, and some items of cabin and ward-room furniture. Waiting for him was the temporary commanding officer, Lieutenant W. W. Carnes, seven men, one boy, and one servant.

In its prime the *Water Witch* had carried two smooth-bore twelve pounders, a thirty pounder, and a twelve-pounder rifle. With a length of 150 feet, it was classed as a side-wheel sloop. It was built in 1852 using a five-year-old Isherwood engine from a previous ship of the same name. Supposedly it was capable of driving the *Water Witch* at eleven and a half knots.[1] The sloop had been in the fray at Head of the Passes against the *Manassas* back in October 1861 and on blockading duty ever since. It was past its prime in Ossabaw Sound. Warley's challenges were to make a channel up the Skidaway River to the Savannah River so he could join the fleet. Once through the narrows, he would have to restock the ship with guns and other heavy gear, build a crew, and keep it healthy.

Warley's first lieutenant was George W. Gift, who had proven himself in combat aboard the *Arkansas* in July 1862 with Isaac Smith and Charles W. "Savez" Read in their epic traverse of the Federal Mississippi fleet. Gift had further distinguished himself in small-boat expeditions, in the mission that destroyed the USS *Underwriter* in New Bern, North Carolina, and in action near Apalachicola, Florida, earlier in the year. If Gift had a weakness, it was including too much information in letters to his wife, which he certainly never expected might fall into enemy hands or even to be read decades later by historians.

It took a week for the new commander to assess the situation and begin besieging Commodore Hunter with requests for men, especially qualified engineers ("of the four firemen sent on board there is not one who has ever fired with coal"), arms, and even a lead line, which had disappeared before Warley's arrival. Hunter sent a group of men under Master H. L. Vaughan. Warley had hoped to bring the ship into Savannah in three weeks, but without army cooperation in digging a channel, that was not to be. By July 16 he was fed up and complained to Hunter about the removal of his medical officer, the want of supplies, the lack of a canal in which move the ship, and the fact that the sheriff told him the ship was in the hands of civil authority. He also encloses a request to Captain Lee at the Bureau of Orders and Details, asking to be detached from a ship that "under the best circumstances can only be to make a show prize vessel in the harbor of Savannah."[2]

The USS *Water Witch* before its capture by Confederate naval forces in June 1864. From U.S. Navy Department, *Official Records of the Union and Confederate Navies, 1894–1922.*

Hunter sent a heated reply informing Warley, "That you are not now in command of an armed vessel ready for service is no fault of mine."[3] This rebuke drew an equally offended reply from Warley.

Aware of this exchange, Gift wrote his wife that he expected to receive command of *Water Witch* within the month. Gift had been spending time with a launch and men mining the backwater approaches to Savannah. A week after the exchange between his superiors, Gift wrote that Flag Officer Hunter was "a poor miserable old brainless nothing, who has no ideas of government of men or officers, but his leading idea is to say 'no' before he hears your story." Notwithstanding this judgment of Hunter's character, Gift thought that Hunter liked him and might appoint him his flag lieutenant, or at least give him command of a fleet of torpedo boats. Job opportunities abounded, at least in the mind of Lieutenant Gift.[4]

Even as Gift was writing his analysis of his commodore, attempts were made toward freeing the *Water Witch* so it could join the Savannah Fleet. Hunter sent a pilot for "Skidaway Narrows" to Warley and asked the navy for permission to seek local help in making a channel for the vessel. He expected "every day authority from the honorable Navy Department to contract for the making of the channel alluded to. I see no hope of getting the work done by the Army. P.S. We must rely on our own efforts to extricate the *Water Witch*. Let us show the Army we can do it."[5]

Simultaneously Hunter was forwarding (with his approval) an application for command of *Water Witch* by Commander Joseph Price, who had succeeded Lieutenant Pelot and had just been meritoriously promoted after his actions in the taking of the ship and removing it upriver. The application was rejected by the Navy Department, which declined to remove Warley from command.

Warley remained positive and, recognizing a kindred spirit of adventure in young Gift, told him to "propose something startling." Warley had private funds for independent enterprises from his Wagner kinfolk in Charleston[6] and thought that small boat raids were among the last avenues to achievement left for the Confederate navy. Gift's enthusiasm for risk had been curbed by his recent marriage, and the proposal did not develop. The month of August went by without a channel, without movement, and without progress of almost any kind.

Far up the Roanoke River in North Carolina was another gunboat, the *Albemarle*—ironclad, battle tested, and leaking. Its captain, Commander John N. Maffitt, was eager to return to the sea. The navy was taking much of the blockade-running business into its own hands, and Maffitt was too valuable not to use. He was detached from the *Albemarle,* and on September 9, Alex Warley received orders forwarded by Hunter "from the Honorable Navy Department," detaching Warley from command of the *Water Witch* and having him turn over command to Master H. L. Vaughan. Subsequent orders directed Warley to proceed to Plymouth, North Carolina, to take command of the steamer *Albemarle* "without delay."

Books have been devoted to the *Albemarle.* It was built in a cornfield at Edward's Ferry, near Scotland Neck, North Carolina, by a pair of young ship contractors and commissioned in April 1864. On its shakedown cruise down the Roanoke, it met and defeated the Federal fleet at Plymouth and it later took part in a major conflict in Albemarle Sound. Warley was setting out to participate in the final chapter of the famous two-gun steam sloop, just commissioned five months earlier.

James W. Cooke, lately called "Ironmonger Captain" for his determination in procuring sheathing for his craft, had brought *Albemarle* down the Roanoke, still under construction and with gunners who learned the drill of both 6.2-inch Brooke rifles while the armor plates were still being bolted down and while navigating a tricky river. Cooke had taken it to the sound and twice defeated all comers, including seven on the second occasion. He had regained the town of Plymouth, but then illness forced him out for a while, and Maffitt had arrived.

Maffitt found himself with the most formidable two-gun warship in the North Carolina sounds. While it had many weaknesses and flaws, these

The North Carolina sounds. The CSS *Albemarle* protected Plymouth
on Albemarle Sound. From Century Magazine, *Battles and Leaders
of the Civil War,* 1887–90.

problems were not known to the Federals. They knew only that destroying
the *Albemarle* was the key to taking Plymouth and controlling much of the
breadbasket of eastern Carolina. They had done their best off Sandy Point
on May 5, 1864, and had been bested. They had, however, stopped the *Albemarle* on its mission across the sound. Two ironclads might well have their
way with the wooden enemy, but the *Neuse,* the *Albemarle*'s sister ship, was
stranded in Kinston.

If the *Albemarle* were lost, so too would be Plymouth and eastern North Carolina. The risk of loss increased with the exposure of cruising. Immediately Southern ground forces judged the safety of Plymouth to outweigh any spoils of enemy gunboats. This feeling was shared by Commodore Pinckney upriver in Halifax and by Captain Cooke. But these judgments went against the fighting nature of Maffitt, who was buoyed by the verbal orders of Secretary Mallory to "attack the enemy's fleet in the sound with the *Albemarle*."[7]

Maffitt took the ship to the mouth of the river often in August and usually in the dead of night. He was tempted out into the sound by the Federal picket boats but did not take the bait. Mallory had amplified his "attack orders" with language designed to remind everyone of the importance of *Albemarle* to the entire region; yet he still left the decision of combat in the hands of the naval commanders on the scene. Another complication was the increased leaking of his hull. In the haste that accompanied most Confederate shipbuilding, the lumber cut for the hull was not cured. Any structure built of green lumber will change shape as it cures.[8]

In part to relieve the tedium, Maffitt organized boat raids on the sounds, with varying success, until the second week of September 1864, when he received orders to Wilmington. He was to take command of a blockade-runner, the *Owl*.

As Maffitt was working his way from Plymouth to Wilmington, Warley was making the tortuous rail trip from Savannah to Charleston to Raleigh. It was September and hot. The train was traveling at ten miles per hour and making many stops for maintenance. Warley was sure he was leaving a dead-end assignment, and the exploits of the *Albemarle* were well known—far better known than its current condition and mission. He thought he would be working for Captain R. F. Pinckney in Halifax, North Carolina. He was not aware that, while he was in transit, Pinckney was being relieved by Cooke, who had been meritoriously promoted to captain the previous June in recognition for his successful battles in the *Albemarle*.

On arrival at Plymouth, Warley found the most powerful gunboat on the sounds to be secured to the waterfront. The crew numbered about sixty, many sick, and the ship was showing its shortcomings in many small ways. For example the crew slept in plank bunks because of a shortage of cloth for hammocks.[9] This did not bother the crew, however, because most of them were landsmen, and the concept of hammocks was completely foreign to them.

To see what he had to work with and keep the Federals on edge, Warley took the *Albemarle* out to the mouth of the river at noon on September 23 and did a grand promenade, sending the USS *Valley City* to general quarters and skittering out into the sound while firing a signal gun. The gun drew a crowd of Federal vessels, which came to the Roanoke River and steamed about until six in the evening, when they realized the *Albemarle* had returned home and would not be seen again that day.[10]

Warley had settled into the realization that his crew was too small and often sick "with the ague." While he had confidence in them, he had little or none in the army personnel assigned to guard his craft and their town: "The guns commanding the river were in no condition for use, and the troops in charge of them were worn down by ague, and were undrilled and worthless." He sent out ten of his crew at all times to forage some and harass the enemy.[11] These efforts gained some appreciation from army authorities.

Perhaps unknown, but certainly suspected by the Confederates, were the periodic reconnaissance parties of Federal sailors, who would bring a small boat up the Middle River and cut through the swamp to the far bank of the Roanoke to observe the state of things at the Plymouth waterfront. A mile downstream from Plymouth, they noticed the condition of the wreck of the *Southfield,* which they supposed would be raised to work in concert with the *Albemarle,* and they were surprised at the general inactivity there. They counted the sentries in the town and on the ship. In September they had noted a ring of cypress logs, held at log's length around the perimeter of the ironclad's moorage.

That ring of logs was designed to prevent ramming by explosive devices, the development of which had become a Confederate specialty. Imitation, the sincerest form of military retribution, had been planned since midsummer, when Lieutenant Will Cushing of the U.S. Navy had proposed a torpedo-boat attack on the *Albemarle.*

The twenty-three-year-old Cushing had made his name in boat raids in coastal North Carolina, capturing people and positions and conducting reconnaissance against all odds. It was his reputation that had sold the plan to outfit two steam launches with howitzers and spar torpedoes, although his squadron commander, Rear Admiral David Porter, wrote with characteristic pessimism to Captain W. H. Macomb, commanding in the sound: "I have directed Lieutenant Cushing to go down in a steam launch, and if possible destroy this ram with torpedoes. I have no great confidence in his success, but you will afford him all the assistance in your power, and keep boats ready to pick him up in case of failure."[12]

It had been Cushing's plan to attack with two launches, preferably landing ashore, capturing the ram, cutting it out from shore, and floating it downriver until they could get motive power. Failing that, he had wanted two shots at torpedoing the hull. The loss of one launch in the Chesapeake dented his plan but did not derail it. "Impossibilities are for the timid: we are determined to overcome all obstacles." Grounding of Cushing's launch on the night of October 26 delayed the attack, and word came to Warley of a steam launch on the river. He informed the commanding army officer of this situation and at the same time warned him that the safety of the place depended on the *Albemarle* and that the safety of the *Albemarle* depended on the watchfulness of the army pickets. Warley was furnished a picket of twenty-five soldiers under a lieutenant who brought rockets and a light fieldpiece. They were stationed downstream near the Southfield, "about a gun-shot below the Albemarle," on the night of the twenty-seventh.[13]

At three in the morning on the twenty-eighth, in poor visibility and swept by rain, Cushing and fourteen others traveled eight miles up the river in a launch with a muffled engine to Plymouth, where the opposite shore, some 150 yards distant, was far away enough to mask the intruders. The picket missed them, but a watch on the *Albemarle* saw "something" and called out.

The hail from the sentry immediately destroyed Cushing's hope of capturing the ship. He now knew he had to sink it. As he ran in close for a look, the night was suddenly illuminated by a prepared bonfire. He saw the ring of cypress logs. Assuming that they had been in the water long enough to be slimy, he decided to make a direct run to bump up and "slip over into the pen [the ring of logs around the *Albemarle*] with the ram."[14] Now under fire from riflemen atop the *Albemarle*'s casemate, he sheared away from his target and circled back across the river to build speed. He had practiced what he planned to do next. As he was standing in the bow, four light lines led away from him. Two were attached to the boat engineer's ankle and wrist for speed directions. Two went to the torpedo.

A lot could go wrong with just the technical side of this operation. The fourteen-foot spar was footed on a universal joint near the launch's starboard bow and was folded aft for travel. It was now swiveled forward and held in elevation by a halyard running up a short mast and down to a small

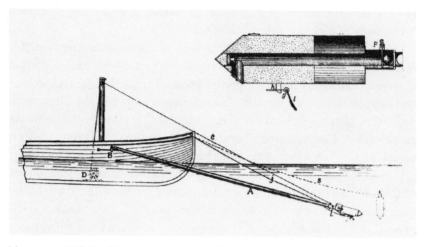

Lieutenant Will Cushing's spar torpedo. The steps required to place the charge were 1) ride up over log boom; 2) drop spar under target's deck; 3) release charge to float up under hull; 4) pull pin to release shot that detonates percussion cap. From Century Magazine, *Battles and Leaders of the Civil War*, 1887–90.

windlass at its foot. A lanyard, held by Cushing, was connected to a pin that held the torpedo to the spar and would gently eject the buoyant casing, powder end down, away from the spar and allow it to float upward to the target hull. His smaller lanyard would pull the pin that would release a grapeshot, which—when the casing was vertical—would fall down upon a percussion cap that would explode and ignite the powder charge. Before this could happen, the launch and spar had to be over the log barrier, and the spar had to be under the ram, then the first lanyard could release the torpedo and allow it to float up to where the second small line would pull the trigger on the percussion cap.

The success of this complex procedure depended on Cushing's being alive at the point of impact. That he *was* alive then was a miracle. The launch came under small-arms fire as it ranged alongside the *Albemarle*, and as the launch turned away, a load of buckshot carried away the back of his coat. The sole on one of his shoes was shot off. As the launch turned back toward its target, there was a lull in the firing, and the Federal crew was again hailed for identification. Their replies varied from "comical answers" to a load of canister from the bow howitzer. Then the launch struck the log barrier and rode up to the point that Cushing told the man

The sinking of the *Albemarle*. On the steam launch at left, Cushing is shown slipping the spar torpedo under the casemate of the *Albemarle*, whose crew is firing on him with rifles and a cannon loaded with grapeshot. From Century Magazine, *Battles and Leaders of the Civil War*, 1887–90.

at the windlass to let loose. The torpedo-tipped spar fell below the casemate overhang of the *Albemarle*, and Cushing gave a strong pull on the detaching line and waited a moment for the charge to rise before pulling the exploding line with his left hand, just then cut by a bullet. At that instant the *Albemarle*'s bow gun was fired in as low a deflection as possible, throwing one hundred pounds of grapeshot and canister in the general direction of the small craft. On the deck Warley knew the bow gun had fired and also felt "a report as of an unshotted gun, and a piece of wood fell at my feet." He sent the carpenter below to check, directing him to report only to the captain and to say nothing to any one else. The man soon reported a "hole in her bottom big enough to drive a wagon in."[15] The *Albemarle* was settling rapidly to the eight foot depth of the river, with its upper works remaining above water.

Cushing rid himself of his pistol, sword, and shoes and jumped into the river, beginning a two-day escape that was a heroic act unto itself. Two of his men drowned; one other escaped; and eleven were captured. None, amazingly, was killed by the gunfire that riddled the clothes of their commander or by the cannon that wrecked the launch.

As soon as the commotion from the dual explosions died down, Warley heard the cries of "surrender" and ceased firing. He sent out boats to look for survivors and assessed his situation. The ironclad was on the

bottom, at an angle with neither gun trainable for firing. It was out of commission. Praising Cushing highly and saying that "a more gallant thing was
not done during the war," he then turned his attention to the town. Having failed in his attempt to convince the army that the town was basically
indefensible without his ironclad, he "did my best to help defend it."[16] Sal-
vaging what he could from the wreck, he took shells and tackles from the
armament and applied them to the two eight-inch guns commanding the
upper river. His men rebuilt the platforms, sunk obstacles downstream in
the river, and waited for the enemy gunboats. They did not wait long. It
took Cushing all night, the next day, and on to midnight of the following
day to swim and paddle his way to his fleet in a stolen skiff. He announced
the destruction of the *Albemarle,* and after celebratory cheering and rockets, the fleet steamed up to the obstacles in the river, fired a few shots over
the town, and steamed back down again. The next day, October 30, they
came up and concentrated on the guns.

Not wishing to endanger his men any further without good result and
not inviting any more harm on the town, Warley set off a charge in the
Albemarle's casemate, blowing out an entire section. He then spiked all the
guns and sent his men down a ravine to the road. He set off for Halifax as
the Federals occupied the town on the afternoon of October 31.[17]

Warley reported the sad news to Captain Cooke in Halifax, received
back pay, and dried his clothes while the news was transmitted to Richmond. On November 9, Smith Lee sent Warley orders to report to Captain
Pinckney in Wilmington, North Carolina.

He reported to Wilmington on December 16, 1864, just as Sherman
was working his way into Savannah. Three days later the *Water Witch* was
burned and Savannah was taken, joining the list of captured cities with
New Orleans, Pensacola, and Norfolk. Mobile and Richmond were both
sealed off by Federal troops. Wilmington was left in Confederate hands,
but their days there were numbered. The Confederate navy remained in
Charleston and in outposts of ordnance and construction at Selma, Char-
lotte, and Columbus.

Warley did not stay long in Wilmington. There was not much occupation for a ship driver in a navy that had a paucity of ships. The CSS *Chicka-
mauga* was in port, and many of its crew assisted in the defense of Battery
Buchanan and Fort Fisher, but Warley went on to Charleston. He did not
find many more opportunities there, but he was better regarded and closer
to home.

He missed the first attack on Fort Fisher, over Christmas, and was long gone when the fort fell on January 15, 1865. Sherman was moving north from Savannah, and on February 10, there was skirmishing on James Island and inland around Charleston as the Federal right wing moved up the coast. Sherman's huge force was in two sections, causing Confederate speculation about whether his objective was Charleston or Augusta. It was neither. Columbia, in the middle, was the immediate target.

The impending force of Sherman's army and the isolation that it brought convinced Beauregard that he needed to evacuate Charleston. Beauregard could not afford to have his army wrapped up by the Federal advance to North Carolina. General Joe Johnston in the Carolinas needed all the assistance he could get, and Beauregard's small force constituted a significant percentage of the available manpower. On February 17 the evacuation began. Federal observers on Morris Island, who had regularly been reading Southern signals, knew the evacuation was coming but were uncertain of the date. They were, however, poised for action.

Back with Ingraham at the Charleston naval station, Warley was in the process of carrying out the destruction orders when first the *Palmetto State* exploded, then his old command the *Chicora,* and then the newer *Charleston,* dropping hot metal from the monstrous blasts onto neighboring piers. The Charleston Squadron was gone. One spectator, caught in the romantic awe of the moment, saw a perfect image of a palmetto tree in the upward destructive moment of the *Palmetto State.*[18]

Three days after the ships had been destroyed and the city evacuated, Captain Lee issued orders relieving Warley from duty in Charleston and authorized him to join the army. It is doubtful that these orders were delivered. Most of the Confederate navy personnel from Charleston and Wilmington, which was evacuated on February 22, became a naval brigade under Commodore J. R. Tucker and manned the guns at and near Drewry's Bluff, just downriver from Richmond. The capital was evacuated on April 1, and part of the naval brigade, under Rear Admiral Raphael Semmes (also brigadier general) joined the presidential train heading south. They manned gun batteries near Danville, Virginia. Tucker's command, having initially been separated from Drewry's Bluff, had little notice of the evacuation but got away together as part of General Custis Lee's rearguard and fought the "last fight" at Saylor's Creek. The rest of the line had surrendered, but the sailors kept fighting because Tucker had never been in a land battle before and "had supposed that everything was going on well."[19]

Miraculously there was still a Confederate naval station in Augusta, Georgia. There Warley applied for duty to his old and not always friendly commodore, W. W. Hunter, in late April—after the surrender of the Army of Northern Virginia on the ninth and Johnston's surrender to Sherman on the eighteenth. Having problems of his own, Hunter referred Warley to "the Honorable Secretary of the Navy, who, I am informed, is in Washington." On May 8. 1865, Warley was captured at Athens, Georgia, by Federal forces commanded by Brevet Brigadier General W. J. Palmer and paroled on or about the same day.

Epilogue

New Orleans, 1865–1895

THE WAR WAS OVER, and the South was in ruins. Alex Warley's professional career was over too, and his future was linked with the South.

Belle Warley was well connected in New Orleans. His mother and sisters were in Pendleton on what was left of the family farm. He had much to do, and almost no resources. He picked up Belle and their first child, Allen Deas Huger Warley (born in 1864 in Pendleton), and went to New Orleans.

Twenty-five years of naval service prepares one best for service at sea. The doors of the U.S. Navy were of course closed to Warley. Many of his contemporaries turned to farming. James Rochelle spent time with the Peruvian Hydrographical Commission of the Amazon, as did Commodore John Tucker, who, after commanding the combined fleets of Peru and Chile, was the commission's president. Beverly Kennon and young James Morgan were in a group of ten former Confederate and ten former Union officers who served the khedive of Egypt for a time. After nine years as captain of a Pacific Ocean mail steamer, William H. Parker accepted an engineering professorship at the Maryland Agricultural College and later became president. Others took positions as captains of merchantmen, often coastal or bay vessels. Some went into education or business.[1]

Warley decided against a second career at sea. He was twice a hero in New Orleans, and something could be found there. For a time, however, he returned intermittently to try to make something of the family place in Pendleton. The 1870 census lists the forty-seven-year-old farmer A. F. Warley with his mother, wife, and three children. In addition to Allen, Alex and

Belle Warley eventually produced Sophia Maude (born 1866), Arthur Middleton Huger (born 1869, died at twenty months), Theodore Dehon Wagner (born 1875), and Felix (born 1876).

For most of the rest of his life, Warley was the clerk of the Board of Liquidation, City Debt, which encompassed the office of the New Orleans mayor, treasurer, and city comptroller. Warley's house was three blocks from City Hall and was described in his obituary as "the big mansion at the corner of Julia and St. Charles Streets, designated as No. 195, that is full of history incidental to the war." What this flattering obituary on the front page of the *Daily Picayune* did not relate was that Belle often took in boarders and money was always short. An undated letter from Belle to William Porcher Miles was wonderfully direct: "I want four hundred dollars in a lump so ask you to lend it to me now." She explained that she spent their savings on the boys' education and that "Aleck has become such a complete invalid that I worry him with nothing."[2] The hero of the *Manassas* had not, however, been let down by the city. He still retained his clerkship to the end.

On his death in his home at 195 St. Charles Street on January 12, 1895, the seventy-two-year-old was treated well in the modest manner he had requested. He went home by train to Pendleton for the last time and was laid to rest in the churchyard of St. Paul's Episcopal Church. Belle lived until January 11, 1924, dying at age eighty-seven in Houston, Texas. She is buried with her family in Mobile.

Appendix 1

Naval Ranks, Positions, and Titles

For those not familiar with the U.S. Navy, the tangle of ranks and titles is a constant confusion. Officers of one rank are often referred to by another. Many times this usage is correct, and even military historians can become confused. Officer ranks in the U.S. Navy until 1862 were as follows:

acting midshipman (warranted)
midshipman (warranted)
passed midshipman (warranted)
master (warranted)
lieutenant (commissioned)
commander (commissioned)
captain (commissioned)

A commission, technically awarded by the president, allowed one to command. A warrant, given by the secretary of the navy, demonstrated "trust and confidence," but did not allow command. Staff officers (such as engineers and paymasters), boatswains (bosuns), gunners, and others who had risen through the ranks were warranted along with midshipmen, passed midshipmen, and masters.

There were no admirals because that rank was considered somewhat pretentious. Congress, which allowed only six army generals until the start of the Civil War, saw no use in overloading the navy with rank. There were also no medals or personal decorations—generally as a rejection of European values.

The confusion in regard to navy officers is caused by the fact that the person commanding a vessel is the captain, and is addressed as such regardless of his actual rank. Thus a commander or a lieutenant can be addressed as "captain." During Warley's service in the U.S. Navy, captains usually commanded frigates and ships of the line; commanders took sloops and supply vessels; and lucky lieutenants had schooners, sometimes storeships.

All these officers were called "captain." A lieutenant with a ship was also termed "lieutenant commanding" for as long as he had the job, which provided a conditional elevation and an increase in pay. Historians have sometimes erroneously referred to lieutenants commanding as "lieutenant commanders."

The second senior officer of a ship's company is now called the executive officer and is sometimes addressed as "commander," regardless of rank. In the midnineteenth century, a commander might be aboard a ship of the line, reporting to the captain. In most cases, however, the other officers were lieutenants, and the senior lieutenant was the first lieutenant (executive officer) and was called "number one" or "the luff."

An officer commanding a squadron or collection of ships was (and still is) called the "commodore" and flew a broad pennant from his ship. This practice came from the Royal Navy line-of-battle days when a fleet formed in three sections with the admiral in command with his flag in the center, the second senior admiral in the van (or lead section) with his flag, and the junior admiral in the third section with his. Thus came the relative ranks of admiral, vice (van) admiral, and rear admiral. These ranks took some time to cross the ocean to the U.S. Navy. Beginning in 1857, the commodore was also called the flag officer for the obvious reason, and was addressed as such, including in official correspondence. Revisions in 1862 created the rank of rear admiral. Vice admiral came in 1864 and admiral in 1866.

On completion of a command, an officer reverted to his official rank again, but courtesy titles often continued unofficially. Years after the Civil War, Warley, though never promoted above lieutenant, was always referred to as "captain" for his command of warships.

This rank structure was continued in the Confederate navy, which specified equivalents in army rank:

passed midshipman	second lieutenant
master	first lieutenant
lieutenant	captain
lieutenant commanding	major
commander	lieutenant colonel
captain	colonel
rear admiral	major general

The Confederate navy split lieutenants into second and first, with the junior grade established as a temporary rank for the duration of the war.

Masters were designated "in line of promotion" or "not in line," denoting a sort of limited-duty officer status.

In 1862 the U.S. Navy commissioned ranks were expanded beyond the warranted midshipman (who remained at that rank after graduation from the Naval Academy for as long as a year until he passed his examination). The new ranks were

ensign
master (later lieutenant, junior grade)
lieutenant
lieutenant commander
commander
captain
commodore
rear admiral

The rank of commodore disappeared in 1899 and reappeared briefly during World War II. It emerged again in the 1980s, when the navy was required to institute a one-star rank to match the other services in appearance as well as in pay. The titles of commodore and commodore admiral were tried before the return to rear admiral (lower half) in 1985. Official ranks are now:

ensign
lieutenant (junior grade)
lieutenant
lieutenant commander
commander
captain
rear admiral (lower half)
rear admiral (upper half)
vice admiral
admiral

Appendix 2

The Warley Family

Children of Colonel Jacob Warley and Sophia Fraser Warley

1. Son, b. October 25, 1816; d. in infancy.
2. Sophia Mills, b. December 10, 1817; d. in infancy.
3. Jacob William, b. October 25, 1819; d. November 25, 1843.
4. Alexander Fraser, b. September 12, 1821; d. in infancy.
5. Alexander Fraser, b. July 29, 1823; d. January 13, 1895; m. (1) Emily Forrest, June 13, 1850; (2) Isabella Middleton Huger, December 1, 1862.
6. Sophia Miles, b. February 17, 1825; d. November 25, 1893; m. Theodore Dehon Wagner (widower of sister Sarah Ella Warley), October 1, 1874.
7. Elizabeth Georgiana Taylor, b. December 31, 1827; d. February 29, 1884; m. (1) Henry Hamilton Schulz, June 20, 1850; (2) Charles James Bourn, August 25, 1859.
8. James Hamilton, b. November 6, 1828; d. May 31, 1884.
9. Frederick Fraser, b. August 28, 1830; d. April 15, 1875; m. Rowena Law, July 8, 1852.
10. Sarah Ella, b. January 26, 1833; d. February 16, 1863; m. Theodore Dehon Wagner, January 19, 1860.
11. Anna Richardson, b. January 26, 1833; d. September 24, 1898; m. John Hanscame Holmes, October 21, 1852.
12. Felix, b. January 1, 1835; d. February 25, 1905.

The genealogy for this first generation is on file at the South Carolina Historical Society in Charleston.

Children of Lieutenant Alexander Fraser Warley and
Isabella Middleton Huger Warley

Belle Warley was born in Mobile, Alabama, in 1836, the daughter of Colonel John Middleton Huger (pronounced "u gee") a native of Charleston, South

Carolina, and connected to the oldest families in South Carolina, as was his wife, who was a Deas (pronounced "days"). Belle Warley died on January 11, 1924, and was buried in the family vault in Mobile. Children:

1. Allen Deas Huger, b. 1864.
2. Sophia Maude, b. 1866; m. John Hunter.
3. Arthur Middleton Huger, b. 1869; d. May 1871.
4. Theodore Dehon Wagner, b. 1875.
5. Felix, b. 1876, d. 1935.

While the census of 1870 lists the Warley family in Pendleton, South Carolina, New Orleans city directories in the 1880s and 1890s indicate that the family lived at 195 St. Charles Street, just two blocks from the old city hall. Street renumbering in 1894 shifted the address to 780 St. Charles. Sons Allen and Theodore are listed as clerks and bookkeepers—and Allen briefly as an insurance agent—for several New Orleans companies.

Notes

Prologue

1. Log entry, USS *Yorktown*, December 25, 1840, National Archives, Record Group (hereafter NA, RG) 45.
2. Warley family archives, South Carolina Historical Society, Charleston, S.C.

1. First Tour

1. Delaney, *John McIntosh Kell of the Raider* Alabama, 12.
2. Chapelle, *The History of the American Sailing Navy*, 402.
3. Parker, *Recollections of a Naval Officer*, 54.
4. Log entry, USS *Yorktown*, January 4, 1841, NA, RG 45. All subsequent citations of specific dates for ship movements are taken from the various ships' logs.
5. Nordhoff, *Man-of-War Life*, 101.
6. Ibid., 118.
7. Ibid., 214.
8. Alan Villiers's *Captain James Cook* and Charles Nordhoff and James Norman Hall's *Mutiny on the Bounty* both describe Tahiti in evolution from 1769 (Cook's second voyage) to its condition during the *Bounty*'s visit in 1789. The Tahitians had become more savvy with each European visitation and also less numerous because of foreign illness. The population of Tahiti dropped from an estimated high of fifty thousand in 1767 to sixteen thousand in 1797 and to as low as six thousand in the early nineteenth century. The year after the *Yorktown*'s 1841 visit, Tahiti became a French protectorate and was annexed to France in 1843.
9. Chapelle, *The History of the American Sailing Navy*, 330.
10. Ibid., 397.
11. Gapp, "The 'Capture' of Monterey in 1842," 46.
12. Ibid., 49.
13. Ibid., 49–50.
14. Valle, *Rocks and Shoals*, 80.

2. Second Tour

1. Chapelle, *The History of the American Sailing Navy*, 324, 457.
2. Roscoe and Freeman, *Picture History of the U.S. Navy*, fig. 437.

3. Fischer, *Experienced and Conquered*, 187. Fischer was a sixteen-year-old German bandsman who signed on for the three-year cruise. His meticulously kept journal, all in German, presents his perspective of life on a man-of-war.

4. Ibid., 18.

5. National Archives, U.S. Navy Courts-Martial Records, NA, RG 45, roll M-273. All subsequent quotations relating to this court-martial are from this source.

6. Naval History and Heritage Command, *Dictionary of American Naval Fighting Ships* (hereafter *DANFS*).

7. Log entry, USS *Colonel Harney*, August 30, 1845, NA, RG 45.

8. Howarth, *To Shining Sea*, chapter 11.

9. Parker, *Recollections of a Naval Officer*, 130. William Harwar Parker, two years younger and one year junior to Warley, was the son of a captain, Foxhall A. Parker, and younger brother of another officer, who stayed with the North while William went to the South. William Parker's career in both navies paralleled Warley's in many respects. As a passed midshipman, Parker instructed at Annapolis, and his experience led him to command the Confederate Naval Academy.

3. To the Pacific and War

1. Chapelle, *The History of the American Sailing Navy*, 284.

2. Merrill, *Du Pont*, 187.

3. Ibid., 189.

4. Log entry, USS *Independence*, May 10, 1847, NA, RG 45.

5. Amero, "The Mexican-American War in Baja California."

6. Ibid.

7. Warley to Heywood, March 6, 1848, Samuel Francis du Pont Papers, Hagley Museum and Library.

8. Warley to du Pont, March 27, 1848, ibid.

9. Howarth, *To Shining Sea*, chapter 11.

10. Nordhoff, *Man-of-War Life*, 197.

11. Log entries, USS *Independence*, November 4–10, 1848, NA, RG 45.

4. Shore Duty and Back to Sea

1. Herman, *Lighthouse of the Sky*.

2. Ibid.

3. Parker, *Recollections of a Naval Officer*, 82, 86. Parker had observed Forrest under fire at Tabasco in Mexico and described him as a man who "literally did not know the meaning of the word fear." Parker returned home aboard the *Raritan* with Forrest as an outbreak of yellow fever made the ship a floating hospital. He described Forrest's conduct as admirable in example and encouragement.

4. Chapelle, *The History of the American Sailing Navy*, 440.

5. Parker, *Recollections of a Naval Officer*, 33.

6. Log entries, USS *Jamestown,* 1851–52, NA, RG 45.

7. Courts-Martial Records of 1852, National Archives, NA, RG 45.

8. Ibid.

9. Forrest Family Papers, Southern Historical Collection, University of North Carolina, Chapel Hill (hereafter SHC).

10. Tily, *The Uniforms of the United States Navy,* 97–101.

11. Log entry, USS *Savannah,* August 9, 1852, NA, RG 45.

12. Parker, *Recollections of a Naval Officer,* 29.

13. Merrill, *Du Pont,* 217–25.

14. Ibid.

5. BACK TO SEA AND STEAM

1. Log entry, USS *Mississippi,* July 18, 1857, NA, RG 45.

2. Silverstone, *Warships of the Civil War Navies,* 21.

3. Courts-Martial Records, NA, RG 45, M 273, roll 90, January 16, 1858. Subsequent quotations relating to this court-martial are also from this source.

4. Ibid.

5. Merrill, *Du Pont,* 236.

6. Courts-Martial Records, NA, RG 45, M 273, January 18, 1858.

7. Merrill, *Du Pont,* 235.

8. Ibid., 233.

9. Ibid., 237.

10. Ibid., 256–91.

11. Courts-Martial Records, NA, RG 45, M273, roll 91, November 18, 1858. Subsequent quotations relating to this court-martial are from the same source.

12. Merrill, *Du Pont,* 244, and du Pont Papers. Letters from du Pont had constantly referred to Ambassador Reed as a demanding nuisance. The *Minnesota* captain's last word was, "We are all glad to get rid of him, none more than myself." His letters make no reference to his disgraced passenger, Warley.

13. Merrill, *Du Pont,* 244.

6. MAJOR CHANGES

1. Forrest Family Papers, SHC.

2. Scharf, *History of the Confederate States Navy,* 674.

3. Edgar, *South Carolina: A History,* 350.

4. Silverstone, *Warships of the Civil War Navies,* 205.

5. Edgar, *South Carolina: A History,* 352.

6. Rosen, *Confederate Charleston,* 39.

7. William Porcher Miles Papers, SHC.

8. Ibid.

9. Edgar, *South Carolina: A History,* 351.

10. Montgomery, *Columbia, South Carolina,* 46.

11. Edgar, *South Carolina: A History,* 355.

7. ONSET OF HOSTILITIES

1. Burton, *The Siege of Charleston,* 9.

2. Rosen, *Confederate Charleston,* 53.

3. Burton, *The Siege of Charleston,* 38.

4. *Atlas to Accompany the Official Records of the Union and Confederate Armies,* pl. 1.

5. Burton, *The Siege of Charleston,* 40.

6. Coggins, *Arms and Equipment of the Civil War,* 66.

7. Operational Archives, Naval History and Heritage Command, file ZB. Burton, *The Siege of Charleston,* 38.

8. Burton, *The Siege of Charleston,* 38.

9. Ibid., 39.

10. Ibid.

11. Anderson, *By Sea and by River,* 20. Hearn, *The Capture of New Orleans,* 58.

12. Anderson, *By Sea and by River,* 22.

13. Burton, *The Siege of Charleston,* 59.

14. Musicant, *Divided Waters,* 24.

15. Ibid., 25.

16. CSA general order, March 6, 1861, General P. G. T. Beauregard, Operational Archives, Naval History and Heritage Command, file ZB.

8. THE RIVER WAR

1. Morgan, *Midshipman in Gray,* 25. Originally titled *Recollections of a Rebel Reefer,* this memoir was just that, entertaining *recollections* written years after the fact. The significant events were probably etched in Morgan's memory enough to be accurate, but his dates and sequences of events sometimes miss the mark.

2. Ibid., 41.

3. Scharf, *History of the Confederate States Navy,* 272.

4. Warley to Captain E. Higgins, report on Ship Island, *Official Records of the Union and Confederate Armies,* ser. 1, 53:708.

5. Ibid.; also Jones, *The Civil War at Sea,* 1:256.

6. *Official Records of the Union and Confederate Navies* (hereafter ORN), ser. 1, 16:581.

7. Ibid., 15:678.

8. Morgan, *Midshipman in Gray,* 39.

9. Porter was not involved in this action, but always believing that a condemnation of a rival was almost equal to self-promotion, he wrote, "Commander Poor was by no means a staunch loyalist, and actions since the escape of the '*Sumpter*' have

given no proof of energy or zeal in the cause of the Union. He has never, to my knowledge, been under fire nor has he sought in any instance, to place himself where he could do the government the least service" (Hearn, *The Capture of New Orleans*, 43).

10. Ibid., 65.

11. Scharf, *Confederate States Navy*, 112.

12. *ORN*, ser. 2, 1:252–62.

13. Silverstone, *Warships of the Civil War Navies*, 203.

14. Hearn, *The Capture of New Orleans*, 68.

15. Ibid., 74–77.

9. The First Ironclad in Combat

1. Pope to McLean, *ORN*, ser. 1, 16:709–11; "Armament of Gunboats" *ORN*, ser. 1, 17:163.

2. Morgan, *Midshipman in Gray*, 42.

3. The accounts of the battle from the points of view of the participants are slanted and limited to what each individual saw or was able to draw from others. This account was pieced together from the reports in *ORN*, ser. 1, 16:723–30a, including the logs of the USS *Vincennes*, the USS *Water Witch*, and the USS *Nightingale*; articles from the reports of Captain John Pope USN and Lieutenant A. F. Warley CSN; and the commendation letter to Warley from Captain George N. Hollins CSN. Log entries from the mortar schooners and attacking gunboats all give a different time for the movement signal from the flagship. In the absence of a fleet time standard, especially aboard the smaller vessels not likely to carry a chronograph, a variance of up to fifteen minutes is not surprising.

4. Morgan, *Midshipman in Gray*, 43; Hearn, *The Capture of New Orleans*, 89.

5. *ORN*, ser. 1, 16:714.

6. Ibid., 704, 710.

7. Quoted from Jennie Mort Walker, *Life of Captain Joseph Fry: The Cuban Martyr* (Hartford, 1875), in Hearn, *The Capture of New Orleans*, 93.

8. Over the next week, articles in the *New Orleans Daily True Delta*, the *Richmond Dispatch*, and the *Memphis Avalanche* were full of praise, hyperbole, and inaccurate reports about the action. *ORN*, ser. 1, 12:725–30.

9. Morgan, *Midshipman in Gray*, 50.

10. Warley to Miles, February 4, 1862, William Porcher Miles Papers, SHC.

11. Ibid.

12. Pay request, Operational Archives, Naval History and Heritage Command, file ZB.

13. Scharf, *History of the Confederate States Navy*, 243; Miller, *Photographic History of the Civil War*, 218.

14. Pay request, Operational Archives, Naval History and Heritage Command, file ZB.

15. Huger to Miles, March 22, 1862, William Porcher Miles Papers, SHC.

16. Hearn, *Capture of New Orleans*, 168.

17. General orders, *ORN*, ser. 1, 18:48–49.

18. George W. Cable, "New Orleans Before the Capture," in Century Magazine, *Battles and Leaders of the Civil War*, 2:18.

19. Ibid.

20. Hearn, *The Capture of New Orleans*, 174. Barnard's plan was not carried out because of the changes to the forts and because there were no ironclads available.

21. Porter to Welles, April 30, 1862, *ORN*, ser. 1, 18:364. Hearn, *The Capture of New Orleans*, 183.

22. *ORN*, ser. 1, 18:290. Luraghi, *A History of the Confederate Navy*, 159.

23. *ORN*, ser. 1, 18:327–30. It was obvious that the condition and location of the *Louisiana* were the subject of political pressure all the way to President Davis.

24. *ORN*, ser. 1, 18:328.

25. Hearn, *The Capture of New Orleans*, 95.

26. Wilkinson, *The Narrative of a Blockade-Runner*, 24. Wilkinson had served under Farragut in the Mexican War and "knew that Admiral Farragut would dare attempt what any man would." He and Warley did not doubt the Federal commander's intentions or resolve.

10. A Short Night and a Long Morning

1. Hearn, *The Capture of New Orleans*, 220. *ORN*, ser. 1, 18:188–89.

2. *ORN*, ser. 1, 18:303.

3. Ibid., 18:305.

4. Ibid., 18:195, 197, 270; Century Magazine, *Battles and Leaders of the Civil War*, 2:65–66.

5. *ORN*, ser. 1, 18:327.

6. Hearn, *The Capture of New Orleans*, 253. Porter to Fox, May 24, 1862, Fox, *Confidential Correspondence of Gustavus Vasa Fox*, 106,

7. Report of W. C. Whittle, May 24, 1862, *ORN*, ser. 1, 18:314; Porter to Welles, April 30, 1862, ibid., 371; statement of prisoners confined at Fort Warren, Boston Harbor, May 23, 1862, ibid., 317. Those signing the agreement of limited parole of the post were Commander John K. Mitchell, Lieutenant Commanding J. Wilkinson, Lieutenant W. C. Whittle Jr., Lieutenant W. H. Ward, Surgeon J. D. Grafton, Chief Engineer Wilson Youngblood, Second Assistant Engineer James Harris, Second Assistant Engineer M. Parsons, Third Assistant Engineer Joseph Elliott, Second Assistant Engineer Henry Fagan, Third Assistant Engineer John H. Dent, Third Assistant Engineer James H. Tomb, Assistant Paymaster L. E. Brooks, Commodore's Clerk W. B. Clark, Captain's Clerk George Taylor. Signers from the *Manassas* were Lieutenant Commanding A. F. Warley, Lieutenant F. M. Harris, Third Assistant Engineer T. A. Menzies, Second Assistant Engineer Orrin Culver, Third Assistant Engineer William Newman, Second Assistant Engineer George J. Weaver. Not on the original boatload,

but joining the prisoners on board the USS *Colorado* were the following from the army: Captain T. H. Hutton, First Lieutenant B. Dart, Second Lieutenant J. W. Boyle, Lieutenant T. H. Handy, First Lieutenant L. B. Haynes, First Lieutenant William Hervey, Lieutenant O. W. Edwards. Commander Beverly Kennon of the Louisiana navy was a special case, kept along with First Lieutenant Haynes in "close confinement for "very grave charges" unknown to the Confederates. Kennon's restrictions were removed by Navy Secretary Wells on July 3.

8. Porter to Farragut, April 29, 1862, *ORN*, ser. 1, 18:433.

9. Porter to Welles, Porter, *The Naval History of the Civil War*, 223.

10. Farragut to Mitchell, *ORN*, ser. 1, 18:811; Farragut to Trenchard, May 7, 1862, ibid., 18:472.

11. Mitchell to Welles, ibid., 18:313; The USS *Rhode Island* earned her place in history on December 30, 1862: she was towing the USS *Monitor* when the famous ironclad went down off Cape Hatteras.

12. Officers signing the agreement were the following (with asterisks indicating *Manassas* crew members): Commander John K. Mitchell; Lieutenants Commanding J. Wilkinson and *A. F. Warley; Lieutenant W. C. Whittle Jr.; Surgeon J. D. Grafton; Captain T. H. Hutton CSA; First Lieutenant B. Dart CSA; Second Lieutenant J. W. Boyle CSA; Lieutenant T. H. Handy CSA; Lieutenant *F. M. Harris; Assistant Paymaster L. E. Brooks; First Lieutenant L. B. Haynes CSA; First Lieutenant William Hervey CSA; Chief Engineer Wilson Youngblood; Lieutenant O. W. Edwards CSA; Commodore's Clerk W. B. Clark; Commander B. Kennon PNCS (Provisional Navy [of the State of Louisiana in the] Confederate Service); Captain's Clerk George Taylor; Lieutenant W. H. Ward; *Engineer T. A. Menzies; *Engineer Orrin Culver; *Engineer George J. Weaver; *Engineer William Newman; Second Assistant Engineer James Harris; Third Assistant Engineer Joseph Elliott; Second Assistant Engineer Henry Fagan; and Third Assistant Engineers John H. Dent and James H. Tomb.

13. Mitchell to Wells, *ORN*, ser. 1, 18:314; wells to Dimick, ibid., 315 and 317.

14. Dawson, *Sarah Morgan: Civil War Diary of a Southern Woman*, 66.

15. Confederate States Navy Hospital and Prison Records, South Carolina Department of Archives and History, roll 3, sheet 5; *ORN*, ser. 2, 4:438.

16. Morgan, *Midshipman in Gray*, 63, 167. Morgan traveled from New Orleans to Jackson, Mississippi, then to Norfolk and Richmond, before being posted to Drewry's Bluff. He was there for the Federal attack by Rodgers on May 16, 1862. He later related the story of greeting Beverly Kennon on his return from prison.

11. Back to South Carolina

1. *ORN*, ser. 1, 18:343.

2. Officers' orders, Forrest to Warley, August 25, 1862, Operational Archives, Naval History and Heritage Command, file ZB.

3. Captain S. S. Lee to James River Squadron, August 12, 1862, James Henry Rochelle Papers, Perkins Library, Duke University.

4. Coker, *Charleston's Maritime Heritage*, 225.

5. Still, *Iron Afloat*, 82. The State of South Carolina financed the *Palmetto State* until the Confederate government authorized its construction. The South Carolina Executive Committee, then the state government, authorized rolling over the state funds for construction of a second ship, the *Chicora*, and Captain Ingraham helped gain national government approval. The *Chicora* may have benefited from in-state influence in the procurement of timber and other materials.

6. Still, *Iron Afloat*, 87–88; Burton, *The Siege of Charleston*, 125–26.

7. Still, *Iron Afloat*, 115.

8. Rosen, *Confederate Charleston*, 89; Burton, *The Siege of Charleston*, 80–84.

9. Morgan, *Midshipman in Gray*, 73.

10. According to the fourth quarter 1862 payroll for the *Palmetto State* in the National Archives, the relative annual pay for the crew of the Charleston naval station and the *Palmetto State* was as follows:

flag officer	$5,000
lieutenant commanding	$2,550
first lieutenant	$2,100
second lieutenant	$1,700
lieutenant-for-the-war	$1,500
surgeon	$2,000
passed midshipman	$900
midshipman	$550
first assistant engineer	$1,250
second assistant engineer	$1,000
third assistant engineer	$750
gunner	$1,000
assistant paymaster	$1,000

Others were paid monthly at the following rates:

pilot	$100
gunner's mate	$29
coxswain	$28
officers' cook	$26
officers' steward	$25
master's mate	$25
ship's clerk	$24
captain of hold	$24
quarter gunner	$24
seaman	$22
ordinary seaman	$18
landsman	$16

11. Travel voucher, Operational Archives, Naval History and Heritage Command, file ZB.

12. *ORN*, ser. 1, 19:849–50.

13. Ibid.

14. Ibid., 844, 851.

15. Burton, *The Siege of Charleston*, 120–23.

16. Letters from G. H. Bier, NA, RG 45, roll 414.

17. Merrill, *Du Pont*, 288–89.

18. Burton, *The Siege of Charleston*, 140; Parker, *Recollections of a Naval Officer*, 330.

19. Merrill, *Du Pont*, 293; Parker, *Recollections of a Naval Officer*, 330.

20. Porter, *The Naval History of the Civil War*, 185.

21. Mallory to Warley, May 15, 1863, James Henry Rochelle Papers, Perkins Library, Duke University.

22. Burton, *The Siege of Charleston*, 123; Silverstone, *Warships of the Civil War Navies*, 238.

23. *ORN*, ser. 1, 18: 385, 461,593–95.

24. Burton, *The Siege of Charleston*, 231–32. The men from the *Chicora* were Frank Doyle, John Kelly, Michael Caine, and Nicholas Davis. Lieutenant Hasker was taken to the bottom on the fatal dive, his foot trapped in the hatch. He escaped with a broken leg and swam his way up from twenty-four feet.

25. Ibid., 179.

26. Ibid.

27. Scharf, *History of the Confederate States Navy*, 699; Musicant, *Divided Waters*, 401.

28. Scharf, *History of the Confederate States Navy*, 700.

29. *ORN*, ser. 1, 14:608; Burton, *The Siege of Charleston*, 195–96.

30. Musicant, *Divided Waters*, 73–74.

31. Ibid., 74.

32. Pay voucher, May 19, 1864, Operational Archives, Naval History and Heritage Command, file ZB.

12. Two More Commands

1. Silverstone, *Warships of the Civil War Navies*, 24; Naval History and Heritage Command, *DANFS*.

2. *ORN*, ser. 1, 15:746 and 765; Warley to Hunter, July 16, 1864; Hunter to Warley, July 16, 1864; Warley to Hunter, July 18, 1864, Operational Archives, Navy History and Heritage Command, Confed. 67, file ZB. All the letters in this interchange of spirited views did not make it into the *ORN*. The others are in file ZB. The letters indicated that Warley had become restless for action in Charleston and that his posting to an unarmed ship stuck upriver was a condition he wanted immediately rectified. Hunter

pointed out who was in charge and that he, the captain, would not be directed by a lieutenant, especially when neither was completely in control of conditions.

3. Hunter to Warley, July 16, 1864, Operational Archives, Naval History and Heritage Command, file ZB.

4. Gift to wife, July 25, 1864, George W. Gift Papers, SHC.

5. Hunter to Warley, August 25, 1864, *ORN*, ser. 1, 15:765.

6. Gift to wife, July 25, 1864.

7. Elliott, *Ironclad of the Roanoke*, 251–53.

8. Still, *Confederate Shipbuilding*, 59.

9. Warley, note on destruction of the *Albemarle*, Century Magazine, *Battles and Leaders of the Civil War*, 4:641–62.

10. Jones, *The Civil War at Sea*, 3:291.

11. Warley, note on destruction of the *Albemarle*, Century Magazine, *Battles and Leaders of the Civil War*, 4:642.

12. *ORN*, ser. 1, 10:594; Musicant, *Divided Waters*, 419.

13. W. B. Cushing, "The Destruction of the *Albemarle*," Century Magazine, *Battles and Leaders of the Civil War*, 4:635; Warley, note on destruction of the *Albemarle*, 4:642.

14. Cushing, "The Destruction of the Albemarle," 4:637.

15. Warley, note on destruction of the *Albemarle*, 4:642.

16. Ibid.

17. Ibid.

18. Burton, *The Siege of Charleston*, 321.

19. Scharf, *History of the Confederate States Navy*, 749; Parker, *Recollections of a Naval Officer*, 377.

EPILOGUE

1. Scharf, *History of the Confederate States Navy*; Parker, *Recollections of a Naval Officer*; Morgan, *Midshipman in Gray*.

2. William Porcher Miles Papers, SHC.

Bibliography

Manuscript Sources

Confederate States Navy Hospital and Prison Records, South Carolina Department of Archives and History, Columbia, S.C.

Samuel Francis du Pont and Mrs. Samuel Francis du Pont Papers, Hagley Museum and Library, Greenville, Del.

Forrest Family Papers, William Porcher Miles Papers, and George W. Gift Papers, Southern Historical Collection, University of North Carolina, Chapel Hill, N.C.

Officers' Orders, U.S. Ships' Logs, Records of General Courts-Martial and Courts of Inquiry of the Navy Department, Record Group 45, National Archives, Washington, D.C.

Operational Archives, Naval History and Heritage Command, Washington Navy Yard.

James Henry Rochelle Papers, Perkins Library, Duke University, Durham, N.C.

Warley Family Papers, South Carolina Historical Society, Charleston, S.C.

Published Sources

Abdill, George A. *Civil War Railroads.* Seattle: Superior, 1961.

Amero, Richard W. "The Mexican-American War in Baja California." *Journal of San Diego History* 30 (Winter 1984); http://www.sandiegohistory.org/journal/84winter/war.htm (accessed June 10, 2011).

Anderson, Bern. *By Sea and by River: The Naval History of the Civil War.* New York: Knopf, 1962.

Brady, William. *The Kedge-Anchor; or, Young Sailors' Assistant.* New York, 1847. Reprint, Mineola, N.Y.: Dover, 2002.

Brooke, John M. *Ironclads and Big Guns of the Confederacy: The Journal and Letters of John M. Brooke.* Edited by George M. Brooke Jr. Columbia: University of South Carolina Press, 2002.

Burns, Zed H. *Confederate Forts.* Natchez, Miss.: Southern Historical Publications, 1977.

Burton, E. Milby. *The Siege of Charleston 1861–1865.* Columbia: University of South Carolina Press, 1970.

Campbell, R. Thomas. *Academy on the James: The Confederate Naval School.* Shippensburg, Pa.: Burd Street Press, 1998.

Century Magazine. *Battles and Leaders of the Civil War.* 4 vols. New York: Century, 1887–90. Reprint, New York: Appleton-Century-Crofts, 1956.

Chapelle, Howard I. *The History of the American Sailing Navy: The Ships and Their Development.* New York: Norton, 1949.

Chesnut, Mary Boykin. *Mary Chesnut's Civil War.* Edited by C. Vann Woodward. New Haven & London: Yale University Press, 1981.

Coggins, Jack. *Arms and Equipment of the Civil War.* Garden City, N.Y.: Doubleday, 1962.

Coker, P. C., III. *Charleston's Maritime Heritage, 1670–1865: An Illustrated History.* Charleston, S.C.: CokerCraft Press, 1987.

Coski, John M. *Capital Navy: The Men, Ships and Operations of the James River Squadron.* Campbell, Calif.: Savas Woodbury, 1996.

Dawson, Sarah Morgan. *Sarah Morgan: Civil War Diary of a Southern Woman.* Edited by Charles East. New York: Simon & Schuster, 1992.

Delaney, Norman C. *John McIntosh Kell of the Raider Alabama.* Tuscaloosa: University of Alabama Press. 1973.

Dufour, Charles L. *The Night the War Was Lost.* Lincoln: University of Nebraska Press, 1994.

Edgar, Walter. *South Carolina: A History.* Columbia: University of South Carolina Press, 1998.

Elliott, Robert G. *Ironclad of the Roanoke: Gilbert Elliott's Albemarle.* Shippensburg, Pa.: White Mane Books, 1999.

Fischer, Frederick C. *Experienced and Conquered: Aboard USS* Constitution, *1844–1846.* Edited by Annabelle F. Fischer. Translated by Noah G. Good. Westminister, Md.: Peach Originals, 1996.

Foote, Shelby. *The Civil War: A Narrative.* 3 vols. New York: Vintage, 1986.

Fox, Gustavus Vasa. *Confidential Correspondence of Gustavus Vasa Fox: Assistant Secretary of the Navy, 1861–1865.* Edited by Robert M. Thompson and Richard Wainwright. Vol. 2. New York: DeVinne Press, 1919.

Gapp, Frank W. "The 'Capture' of Monterey in 1842." *Naval Institute Proceedings* 105 (March 1979): 46–54.

Hearn, Chester G. *The Capture of New Orleans, 1862.* Baton Rouge: Louisiana State University Press, 1995.

Herman, Jan K. *Lighthouse of the Sky: The U.S. Naval Observatory 1844–1893.* Washington, D.C.: National Academy of Sciences, 1983.

Howarth, Stephen. *To Shining Sea: A History of the United States Navy, 1775–1991.* New York: Random House, 1991.

Jones, Virgil Carrington. *The Civil War at Sea.* 3 vols. New York: Holt, Rinehart & Winston, 1960–62.

Long, E. B. *The Civil War Day by Day: An Almanac, 1861–1865.* Garden City, N.Y.: Doubleday, 1971.

Luraghi, Raimondo. *A History of the Confederate Navy.* Annapolis: Naval Institute Press, 1996.

Melville, Herman. *White-Jacket; or, The World in a Man-of-War.* New York: Harper, 1850.

Merrill, James M. *Du Pont, the Making of an Admiral: A Biography of Samuel Francis du Pont.* New York: Dodd, Mead, 1986.

Miller, David, ed. *The Illustrated Directory of Uniforms, Weapons and Equipment of the Civil War.* London: Salamander Books, 2001.

Miller, Francis Trevelyan, ed. *Photographic History of the Civil War.* Vol. 6: *The Navies.* New York: Yoseloff, 1957.

Morgan, James Morris. *Recollections of a Rebel Reefer.* Boston & New York: Houghton Mifflin, 1917. Abridged edition, *Midshipman in Gray: Selections from Recollections of a Rebel Reefer.* Shippensburg, Pa.: Burd Street Press, 1997.

Musicant, Ivan. *Divided Waters: The Naval History of the Civil War.* New York: HarperCollins, 1995.

Naval History and Heritage Command, *Dictionary of American Naval Fighting Ships;* http://www.history.navy.mil/danfs/ (accessed June 27, 2011).

Nordhoff, Charles [1830–1901]. *Man-of-War Life: A Boy's Experience in the United States Navy, during a Voyage Around the World in a Ship-of-the-Line.* New York: Dodd, Mead, 1855. Reprint, Annapolis: Naval Institute Press, 1985.

Nordhoff, Charles [1887–1947], and James Norman Hall. *Mutiny on the Bounty.* Boston: Little, Brown, 1932.

Page, Dave. *Ships versus Shore: Civil War Engagements along Southern Shores and Rivers.* Nashville, Tenn.: Rutledge Hill Press, 1994.

Parker, William H. *Recollections of a Naval Officer, 1841–1865.* New York: Scribners, 1883.

Porter, David D. *The Naval History of the Civil War.* New York: Sherman, 1886.

Reed, Rowena. *Combined Operations in the Civil War.* Annapolis: Naval Institute Press, 1978.

Ringle, Dennis J. *Life in Mr. Lincoln's Navy.* Annapolis: Naval Institute Press, 1998.

Roscoe, Theodore, and Fred Freeman. *Picture History of the U.S. Navy.* New York: Scribners, 1956.

Rosen, Robert N. *Confederate Charleston: An Illustrated History of the City and the People during the Civil War.* Columbia: University of South Carolina Press, 1994.

Scharf, J. Thomas. *History of the Confederate States Navy from Its Organization to the Surrender of Its Last Vessel,* New York: Rogers & Sherwood, 1887. Reprint, New York: Fairfax Press, 1977.

Silverstone, Paul H. *Warships of the Civil War Navies.* Annapolis: Naval Institute Press, 1989.

Slagle, Jay. *Ironclad Captain: Seth Ledyard Phelps and the U.S. Navy, 1841–1864.* Kent, Ohio & London: Kent State University Press, 1996.

Stern, Philip Van Doren. *The Confederate Navy: A Pictorial History.* Garden City, N.Y.: Doubleday, 1962.

Still, William N., Jr. *The Confederate Navy: The Ships, Men, and Organization, 1861–1865.* Annapolis: Naval Institute Press, 1997.

———. *Confederate Shipbuilding.* Athens: University of Georgia Press, 1969. Reprint, Columbia: University of South Carolina Press, 1987.

———. *Iron Afloat.* Nashville: Vanderbilt University Press, 1971. Reprint, Columbia: University of South Carolina Press, 1985.

Still, William N., Jr., John M. Taylor, and Norman C. Delaney, *Raiders and Blockaders: The American Civil War Afloat.* Washington, D.C. & London: Brassey's 1998.

Tily, James C. *The Uniforms of the United States Navy.* New York: Yoseloff, 1964.

Trotter, William R. *Ironclads and Columbiads: The Civil War in North Carolina, the Coast.* Winston-Salem, N.C.: John F. Blair, 1989.

U.S. Navy Department. *Official Records of the Union and Confederate Navies in the War of Rebellion.* 30 vols. in two series. Washington, D.C.: U.S. Government Printing Office, 1894–1922.

U.S. War Department. *Atlas to Accompany the Official Records of the Union and Confederate Armies.* 2 vols. Washington, D.C.: U.S. Government Printing Office, 1891, 1895.

———. *The War of the Rebellion: Official Records of the Union and Confederate Armies.* 70 vols. in 4 series. Washington, D.C.: U.S. Government Printing Office, 1888–1901.

Valle, James E. *Rocks and Shoals: Order and Discipline in the Old Navy 1800–1861.* Annapolis: Naval Institute Press, 1980.

Villiers, Alan. *Captain James Cook.* New York: Scribners, 1967.

Wideman, John C. *Naval Warfare: Courage and Combat on the Water.* New York: MetroBooks, 1997.

Wiley, Bell Irvin. *Embattled Confederates.* New York: Harper & Row, 1964.

Wilkinson, John. *The Narrative of a Blockade-Runner.* New York: Sheldon, 1877.

INDEX

Page numbers for illustrations are in italics.

About the Author

JOHN M. STICKNEY holds a degree in mechanical engineering from Auburn University and an M.B.A. from the University of South Carolina. A former consulting engineer, Stickney is a retired captain in the U.S. Navy Reserve. He and his wife, Priscilla, have two naval officer sons and a daughter, who is a charter boat captain. They live on a lake near Columbia, South Carolina.